Picture Chord Pocket Guide

INTRODUCTION

The *Picture Chord Pocket Guide* is designed to serve two purposes: first, it's a reference guide to chords; second, it's a collection of popular guitar sounds.

Use it when you're learning a new song and you come across a chord that's unfamiliar to you. Use it when you're composing your own music and looking for "just the right chord." Use it to explore the guitar fretboard, to improve your chord playing, to increase your understanding of chord theory, or just to discover new and unusual sounds. The applications are almost limitless.

The *Picture Chord Pocket Guide* is a comprehensive source for chords, for all playing styles and levels. It contains two easy-to-play voicings of 40 chord qualities for each of the twelve musical keys. All totaled, that's 960 chords right in your pocket! These chords and their fingerings have been chosen for their playability and their practicality, ensuring a wealth of usable fingering for any musical situation.

Enjoy!

ISBN 9

HAL•LEONARD®
CORPORATION
7777 W. BLUEMOUND RD. P.O. BOX 13819 MILWAUKEE, WI 53213

Visit Hal Leonard Online at
www.halleonard.com

HOW TO USE THIS BOOK

The *Picture Chord Pocket Guide* contains 960 chord voicings and over 400 unique chord types. To help you find your way to the chord y need, all the chords are organized first by root (C, C♯, D, E♭, E, etc.) a then by quality or type (major, minor, seventh, etc.)

Each chord is identified by its symbol: **Csus4**

By its full name: **C s**

And by its spelling:

Then, you are given a choice of two voicings, which are presented chord frames and photos. In a chord frame, the six vertical lines repre the six strings on the guitar, from low E to high E, moving left to right. horizontal lines represent the frets:

X's tell you a string should not be played or should be muted.

A dark, thick line represents the **nut** on the guitar.

O's indicate an open str

Black **dots** indicate the notes to be played, as well as their location on the fret-board. **Numbers** tell you what fingers to use to fret the strings. Think of your left-hand fingers as being numbered 1 through 4:

A **barre** (pronounce like "bar") shown whe finger holds down two o more string the same ti

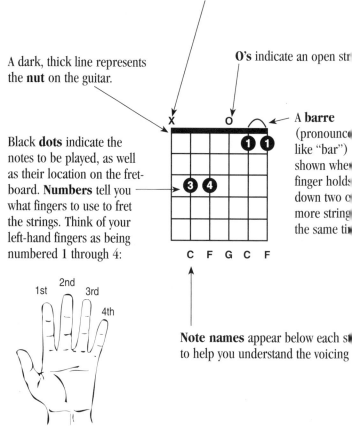

Note names appear below each s to help you understand the voicing

Chords above the fifth fret use a **fret number** (e.g., "5 fr") to the right of the chord frame. This tells you to move your hand up to that fret to position your fingers.

☞ One of the goals of this book is to provide "playable" chord fin gerings. The fingerings in this book were chosen for their ease play and transition between other chords in a progression. However, remember that they are only recommended fingering If you feel more comfortable with an alternate fingering, feel fr to use it. There is no single way to play these chords.

CHOOSING THE BEST VOICING

Any chord can have a number of different voicings. A *voicing* refers
ow the notes of the chord are arranged—which corresponds to where
chord is played on the guitar, and how it's fingered. Each chord quality
his book is presented with two different voicings. Typically, the first
rd voicing presented is in the lowest position on the fretboard. The
er voicing usually appears higher up the neck. Within these voicings,
may encounter open chords, barre chords, broken-set chords, and
acent-set chords:

Open Chords

Open chords occur within the first five frets of
guitar and contain at least one open string. These
rds are often the most appropriate choice for
mming purposes. They're also typically the easi-
voicings to learn when you're a beginner.

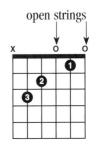

open strings

Barre Chords

Barre chords can occur anywhere on
neck and serve as a type of "all-purpose"
rd voicing; that is, they can be
mmed, plucked, or played fingerstyle,
 can be used in almost any musical
ing.

Barre chords require you to lay a finger flat
oss a fret and press down all the indicated
ngs simultaneously. This can be challenging for
eginning guitarist. If you find these chords to be
ecially difficult at first, don't give up. Just keep
cticing, and be patient.

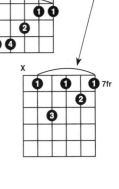

barre

Broken-Set Chords

Broken-set chords also provide good, multi-purpose chord voicings. These chords contain a bass note on the fifth or sixth string and two or three notes on the higher strings, with at least one interior string muted, or not played. These often work best in a jazz or blues setting, especially when playing solo.

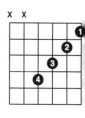

Adjacent-Set Chords

Adjacent-set chords contain notes on the middle or top four strings. These chords also work well within the jazz or blues idioms, especially for chord-melody techniques or when playing with another instrument that provides a bass line.

One thing to remember is that many of these voicings are unique. Open strings are taken advantage of when possible, but many moveable voicings are included as well. So, just because you've learned two moveable shapes for C7, for example, that doesn't mean there aren't any more moveable seventh chord shapes in the book. Usually, you'll find other moveable voicings for the same chord by looking through the other keys throughout the book.

Ultimately, which chord voicing you choose will depend on either your playing level or the situation at hand. Musically speaking, if you're playing a chord sequence high on the neck, a chord voiced down low would probably sound out of place. Likewise, if you're playing a progression of open chords, jumping up high on the neck for a particular chord would likely sound and feel awkward.

That said, you should become familiar with as many voicings of a chord as you can. They do not all sound the same. Practice switching between different voicings of the same chord, and compare how they sound. If you like, go ahead and practice a progression where you jump from high to low on the neck—there really are no rules in music that can't be broken.

CHORD CONSTRUCTION

WHAT'S A CHORD?

In order to effectively choose and utilize the chords in this book, it is important to have a basic understanding of how chords are constructed. So, what is a chord? A chord is simply defined as *three or more notes* played at the same time. Typically, its function is to provide the harmony that supports the melody of a song.

HOW DOES A CHORD GET ITS NAME?

A chord gets its name from its root note. For example, the root of a G major chord is G. The remaining notes in the chord determine its *quality, or type.* This is indicated by the chord suffix. So, in a Bm7♭5 chord, B is the root, and m7♭5 is the suffix that indicates the quality of the chord.

root   quality or type

This book contains 40 chord types. Here is a summary table to help you keep track of the suffix for each chord type:

SUFFIX	CHORD TYPE
no suffix	major
5 (no 3rd)	fifth (power chord)
sus4	suspended fourth
sus2	suspended second
add9	added ninth
6	sixth
6/9	sixth, added ninth
maj7	major seventh
maj9	major ninth
maj7♯11	major seventh, sharp eleventh
maj13	major thirteenth
m	minor
m(add9)	minor, added ninth
m6	minor sixth
m♭6	minor, flat sixth
m6/9	minor sixth, added ninth
m7	minor seventh
m7♭5	minor seventh, flat fifth
m(maj7)	minor, major seventh
m9	minor ninth
m9♭5	minor ninth, flat fifth
m9(maj7)	minor ninth, major seventh
m11	minor eleventh
m13	minor thirteenth
7	dominant seventh
7sus4	seventh, suspended fourth
7♭5	seventh, flat fifth
9	ninth
9sus4	ninth, suspended fourth
7♭9	seventh, flat ninth
7♯9	seventh, sharp ninth
7♭5(♯9)	seventh, flat fifth, sharp ninth
11	eleventh
7♯11	seventh, sharp eleventh
13	thirteenth
13sus4	thirteenth, suspended fourth
+	augmented
+7	seventh, sharp fifth
°	diminished
°7	diminished seventh

HOW DO I BUILD A CHORD?

All chords are constructed using intervals. An *interval* is the distance between any two notes. Though there are many types of intervals, there are only five categories: *major, minor, perfect, augmented,* and *diminished.* Interestingly, the major scale contains only major and perfect intervals:

The major scale also happens to be a great starting point from which to construct chords. For example, if we start at the root (C) and add the interval of a major third (E) and a perfect fifth (G), we have constructed a C major chord.

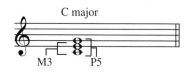

In order to construct a chord other than a major chord, at least one of the major or perfect intervals needs to be altered. For example, take the C major chord you just constructed, and lower the third degree (E) one half step. We now have a C minor chord: C-E♭-G. By lowering the major third by one half step, we create a new interval called a *minor* third.

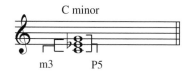

We can further alter the chord by flatting the perfect fifth (G). The chord is now a C°: C-E♭-G♭. The G♭ represents a *diminished* fifth interval.

This leads us to a basic rule of thumb to help remember interval ~~erations:~~

A major interval lowered one half step is a minor interval.

A perfect interval lowered one half step is a diminished interval.

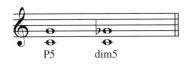

A perfect interval raised one half step is an augmented interval.

☞ Half steps and whole steps are the building blocks of intervals; they determine an interval's quality—major, minor, etc. On the guitar, a *half step* is just the distance from one fret to the next. A *whole step* is equal to two half steps, or two frets.

~~W~~HAT ABOUT OTHER KEYS?

Notice that we assigned a numerical value to each note in the major ~~sc~~ale, as well as labeling the intervals. These numerical values, termed ~~sc~~*ale degrees,* allow us to "generically" construct chords, regardless of ~~ke~~y. For example, a major chord consists of the root (1), major third (3), ~~an~~d perfect fifth (5). Substitute any major scale for the C major scale ~~ab~~ove, select scale degrees 1, 3, and 5, and you will have a major chord ~~fo~~r the scale you selected.

D major scale

Scale degree:	1	2	3	4	5	6	7

Interval:	Root	M2	M3	P4	P5	M6	M7

D major chord

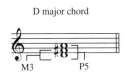

The chart below is a construction summary of the chord types in this book (based on the key of C only) using the scale degree method:

CHORD TYPE	FORMULA	NOTES	CHORD NAME
major	1-3-5	C-E-G	C
fifth (power chord)	1-5	C-G	C5
suspended fourth	1-4-5	C-F-G	Csus4
suspended second	1-2-5	C-D-G	Csus2
added ninth	1-3-5-9	C-E-G-D	Cadd9
sixth	1-3-5-6	C-E-G-A	C6
sixth, added ninth	1-3-5-6-9	C-E-G-A-D	C6/9
major seventh	1-3-5-7	C-E-G-B	Cmaj7
major ninth	1-3-5-7-9	C-E-G-B-D	Cmaj9
major seventh, sharp eleventh	1-3-5-7-♯11	C-E-G-B-F♯	Cmaj7♯11
major thirteenth	1-3-5-7-9-13	C-E-G-B-D-A	Cmaj13
minor	1-♭3-5	C-E♭-G	Cm
minor, added ninth	1-♭3-5-9	C-E♭-G-D	Cm(add9)
minor sixth	1-♭3-5-6	C-E♭-G-A	Cm6
minor, flat sixth	1-♭3-5-♭6	C-E♭-G-A♭	Cm♭6
minor sixth, added ninth	1-♭3-5-6-9	C-E♭-G-A-D	Cm6/9
minor seventh	1-♭3-5-♭7	C-E♭-G-B♭	Cm7
minor seventh, flat fifth	1-♭3-♭5-♭7	C-E♭-G♭-B♭	Cm7♭5
minor, major seventh	1-♭3-5-7	C-E♭-G-B	Cm(maj7)
minor ninth	1-♭3-5-♭7-9	C-E♭-G-B♭-D	Cm9
minor ninth, flat fifth	1-♭3-♭5-♭7-9	C-E♭-G♭-B♭-D	Cm9♭5
minor ninth, major seventh	/1-♭3-5-7-9	C-E♭-G-B-D	Cm9(maj7)
minor eleventh	1-♭3-5-♭7-9-11	C-E♭-G-B♭-D-F	Cm11
minor thirteenth	1-♭3-5-♭7-9-11-13	C-E♭-G-B♭-D-F-A	Cm13
dominant seventh	1-3-5-♭7	C-E-G-B♭	C7
seventh, suspended fourth	1-4-5-♭7	C-F-G-B♭	C7sus4
seventh, flat fifth	1-3-♭5-♭7	C-E-G♭-B♭	C7♭5
ninth	1-3-5-♭7-9	C-E-G-B♭-D	C9
ninth, suspended fourth	1-4-5-♭7-9	C-F-G-B♭-D	C9sus4
seventh, flat ninth	1-3-5-♭7-♭9	C-E-G-B♭-D♭	C7♭9
seventh, sharp ninth	1-3-5-♭7-♯9	C-E-G-B♭-D♯	C7♯9
seventh, flat fifth, sharp ninth	1-3-♭5-♭7-♯9	C-E-G♭-B♭-D♯	C7♭5(♯9)
eleventh	1-5-♭7-9-11	C-G-B♭-D-F	C11
seventh, sharp eleventh	1-3-5-♭7-♯11	C-E-G-B♭-F♯	C7♯11
thirteenth	1-3-5-♭7-9-13	C-E-G-B♭-D-A	C13
thirteenth, suspended fourth	1-4-5-♭7-9-13	C-F-G-B♭-D-A	C13sus4
augmented	1-3-♯5	C-E-G♯	C+
seventh, sharp fifth	1-3-♯5-♭7	C-E-G♯-B♭	C+7
diminished	1-♭3-♭5	C-E♭-G♭	C°
diminished seventh	1-♭3-♭5-♭♭7	C-E♭-G♭-B♭♭	C°7

TRIADS

The most basic chords in this book are called triads. A *triad* is a chord that is made up of only three notes. For example, a simple G major chord is a triad consisting of the notes G, B, and D. There are several types triads, including major, minor, diminished, augmented, and suspended. of these chords are constructed by simply altering the relationships tween the root note and the intervals.

SEVENTHS

To create more interesting harmony, we can take the familiar triad d add another interval: the seventh. Seventh chords are comprised of ur notes: the three notes of the triad plus a major or minor seventh terval. For example, if we use the G major triad (G-B-D) and add a ajor seventh interval (F♯), the Gmaj7 chord is formed. Likewise, if we bstitute the minor seventh interval (F) for the F♯, we have a new seventh ord, the G7. This is also known as a dominant seventh chord, popularly ed in blues and jazz music. As with the triads, seventh chords come in any types, including major, minor, diminished, augmented, suspended, d others.

EXTENDED CHORDS

Extended chords are those that include notes beyond the seventh scale degree. These chords have a rich, complex harmony that is very common in jazz music. These include ninths, elevenths, and thirteenth chords. For example, if we take a Gmaj7 chord and add a major ninth interval (A), we get a Gmaj9 chord (G-B-D-F♯-A). We can then add an additional interval, a major thirteenth (E), to form a Gmaj13 chord (G-B-D-F♯-A-E). Note that the interval of a major eleventh is omitted. This is because the major eleventh sonically conflicts with the major third interval, creating an unpleasant dissonance.

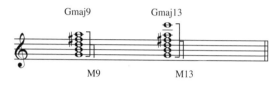

By the way, you may have noticed that these last two chords, Gmaj9 and Gmaj13, contain five and six notes, respectively; however, we only have four fingers in the left hand! Since the use of a barre chord or open string chord is not always possible, we often need to choose the four notes of the chord that are most important to play. The harmonic theory that underlies these choices is beyond the scope of this book, but not to worry—it has already been done for you where necessary. Below are two examples to demonstrate these chord "trimmings."

Generally speaking, the root, third, and seventh are the most crucial notes to include in an extended chord, along with the uppermost extension (ninth, thirteenth, etc.).

IVERSIONS & VOICINGS

This brings us to our last topic. Though a typical chord might consist only three or four notes—a C triad, for example, consists of just a root, rd, and fifth; a G7 chord consists of a root, third, fifth, and seventh— ese notes do not necessarily have to appear in that same order, from ottom to top, in the actual chords you play. Inversions are produced hen you rearrange the notes of a chord:

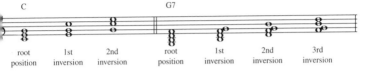

Practically speaking, on the guitar, notes of a chord are often inverted earranged), doubled (used more than once), and even omitted to create fferent voicings. Each voicing is unique and yet similar—kind of like dif- rent shades of the same color.

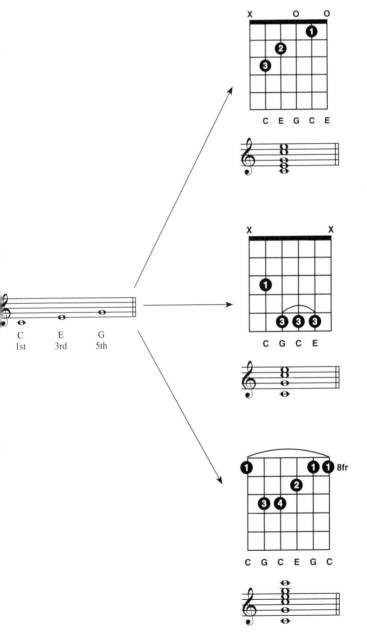

Once again, the possible voicings of a chord are many. The voicings in is book were chosen because they are some of the most popular, useful, d attractive chord voicings playable on the guitar.

C (Cmaj)
C major

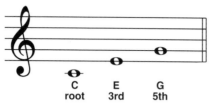

C   E   G
root   3rd   5th

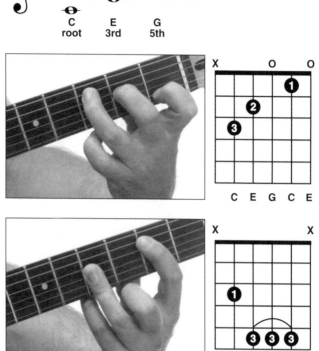

C E G C E

C G C E

C5 (C (no 3rd))
C fifth (power chord)

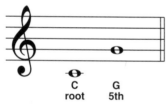

C   G
root   5th

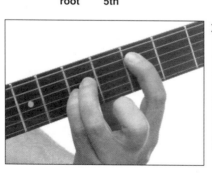

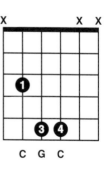

C G C

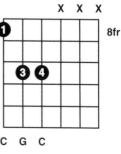

8fr

C G C

Csus4 (Csus)

C suspended fourth

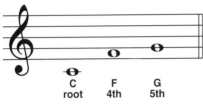

C root | F 4th | G 5th

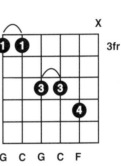

C F G C F

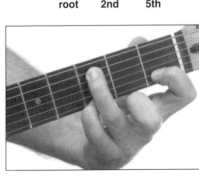
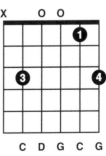

G C G C F

Csus2 (C5add2)

C suspended second

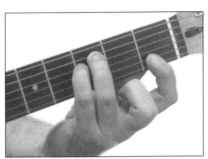
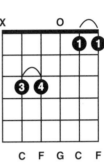

C root | D 2nd | G 5th

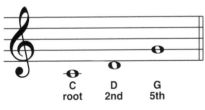

C D G C G

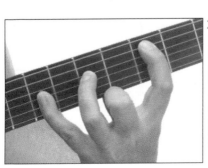
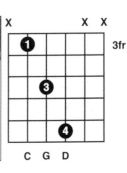

C G D

Cadd9
C added ninth

C	E	G	D
root	3rd	5th	9th

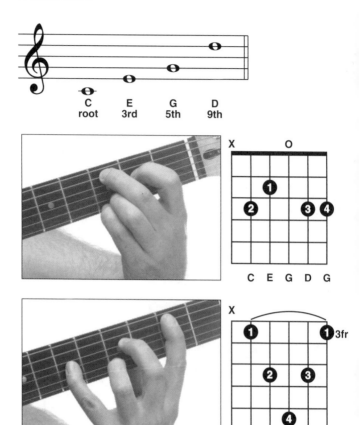

C E G D G

C G D E G

C6
C sixth

C	E	G	A
root	3rd	5th	6th

C E A C E

C A E G

C6/9 (C6add9)
C sixth, added ninth

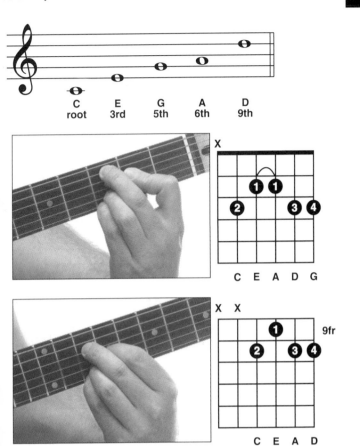

C	E	G	A	D
root	3rd	5th	6th	9th

C E A D G

9fr

C E A D

Cmaj7 (CM7)
C major seventh

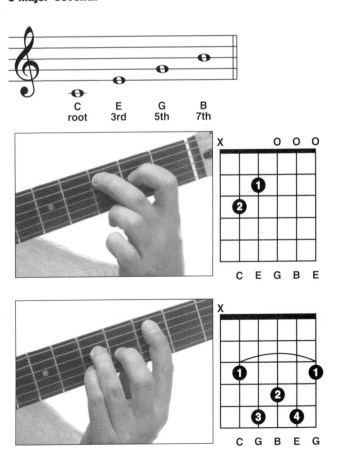

C	E	G	B
root	3rd	5th	7th

C E G B E

C G B E G

Cmaj9 (CM9)
C major ninth

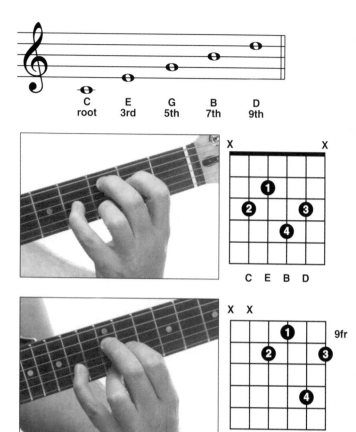

C	E	G	B	D
root	3rd	5th	7th	9th

X   X

C   E   B   D

X   X

9fr

C   E   B   D

Cmaj7#11 (CM7#11)
C major seventh, sharp eleventh

C	E	G	B	F#
root	3rd	5th	7th	#11th

X   O   O

C   E   G   B   F#

X

C   F#   B   E   G

Cmaj13 (CM13)
C major thirteenth

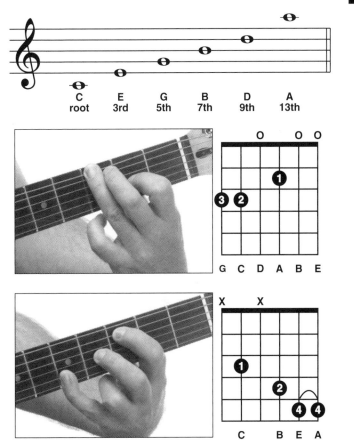

C	E	G	B	D	A
root	3rd	5th	7th	9th	13th

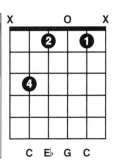

G C D A B E

X X

C B E A

Cm (Cmin, C-)
C minor

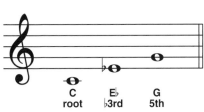

C	E♭	G
root	♭3rd	5th

X O X

C E♭ G C

X

C G C E♭ G

Cm(add9)
C minor, added ninth

C root   E♭ ♭3rd   G 5th   D 9th

C E♭ G D G

8fr

C E♭ G D

Cm6 (Cmin6, C-6)
C minor sixth

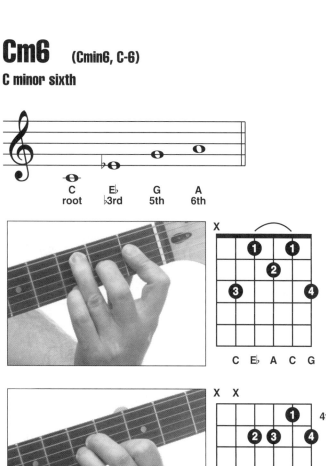

C root   E♭ ♭3rd   G 5th   A 6th

C E♭ A C G

4fr

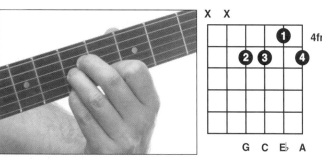

G C E♭ A

Cmᵇ6 (C-(ᵇ6), Cminᵇ6)

C minor, flat sixth

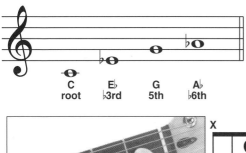

C	Eᵇ	G	Aᵇ
root	ᵇ3rd	5th	ᵇ6th

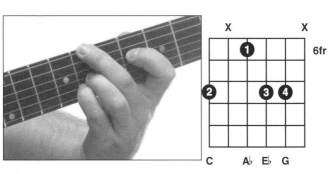

Cm6/9

C minor sixth, added ninth

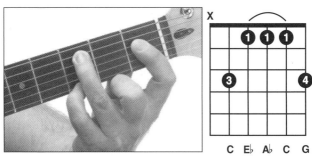

C	Eᵇ	G	A	D
root	ᵇ3rd	5th	6th	9th

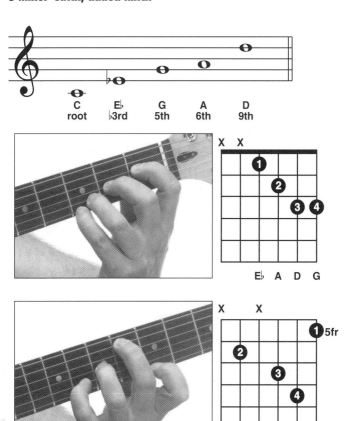

Cm7 (Cmin7, C-7)

C minor seventh

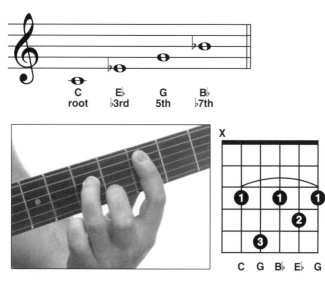

C	E♭	G	B♭
root	♭3rd	5th	♭7th

Cm7♭5 (C-7(♭5), Cmin7-5)

C minor seventh, flat fifth

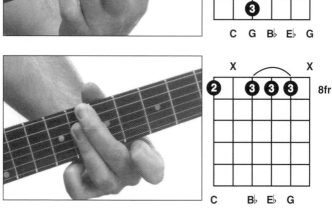

C	E♭	G♭	B♭
root	♭3rd	♭5th	♭7th

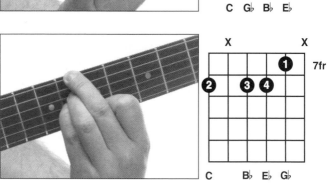

Cm(maj7) (Cm(+7))

C minor, major seventh

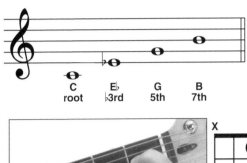

C	E♭	G	B
root	♭3rd	5th	7th

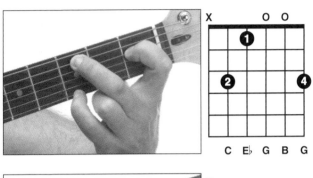

C E♭ G B G

C G B E♭ G

Cm9 (Cmin9, C-9)

C minor ninth

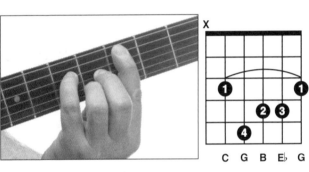

C	E♭	G	B♭	D
root	♭3rd	5th	♭7th	9th

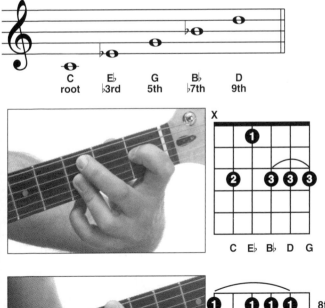

C E♭ B♭ D G

8fr

C G B♭ E♭ G D

Cm9♭5 (Cm9-5, Cmin9♭5)
C minor ninth, flat fifth

C root | E♭ ♭3rd | G♭ ♭5th | B♭ ♭7th | D 9th

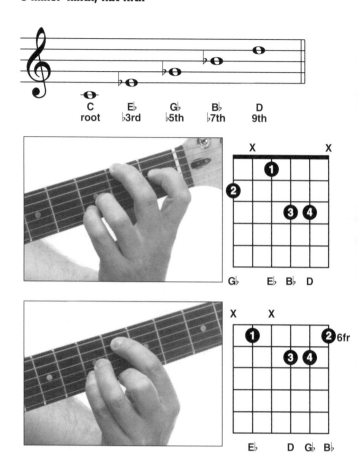

Cm9(maj7) (Cm9+7, C-9+7)
C minor ninth, major seventh

C root | E♭ ♭3rd | G 5th | B 7th | D 9th

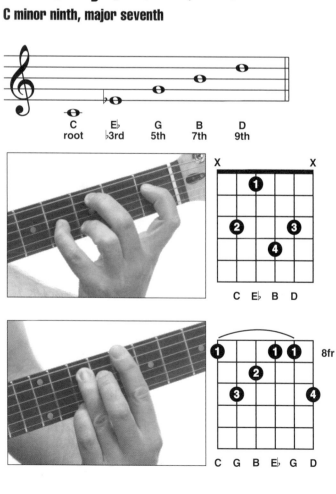

Cm11 (C-11, Cmin11)
C minor eleventh

C	E♭	G	B♭	D	F
root	♭3rd	5th	♭7th	9th	11th

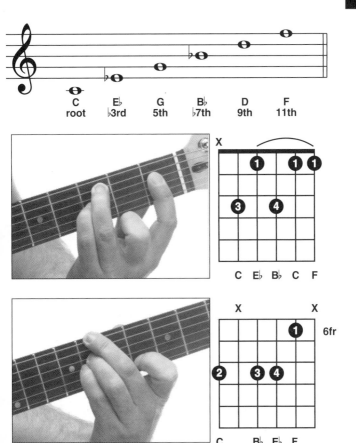

C Eb Bb C F

X **X** 6fr

C Bb Eb F

Cm13 (C-13, Cmin13)
C minor thirteenth

C	E♭	G	B♭	D	A
root	♭3rd	5th	♭7th	9th	13th

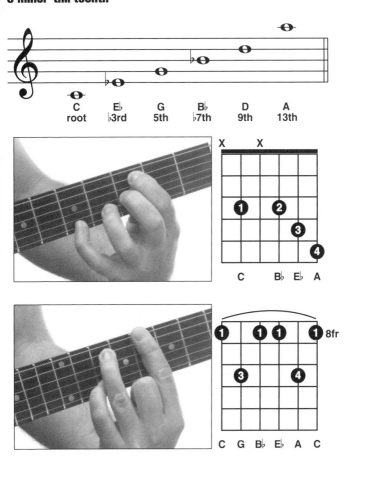

C Bb Eb A

8fr

C G Bb Eb A C

C7 <small>(Cdom7)</small>

C dominant seventh

C	E	G	B♭
root	3rd	5th	♭7th

C E B♭ C E

C G B♭ E G

C7sus4 <small>(C7sus)</small>

C dominant seventh, suspended fourth

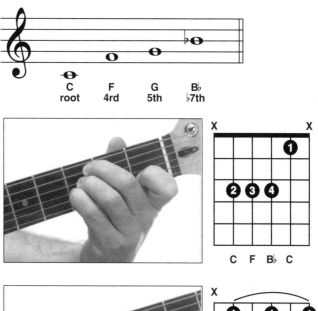

C	F	G	B♭
root	4th	5th	♭7th

C F B♭ C

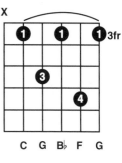

3fr

C G B♭ F G

C7♭5 (C7-5, Cdom7♭5)
C dominant seventh, flat fifth

C	E	G♭	B♭
root	3rd	♭5th	♭7th

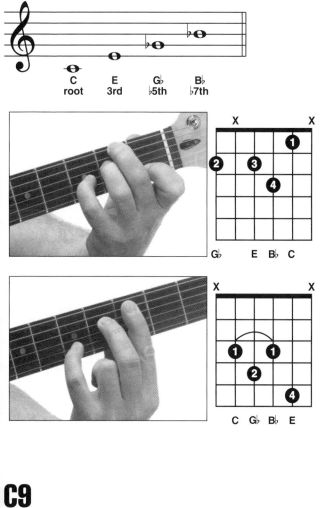

G♭ E B♭ C

C G♭ B♭ E

C9
C ninth

C	E	G	B♭	D
root	3rd	5th	♭7th	9th

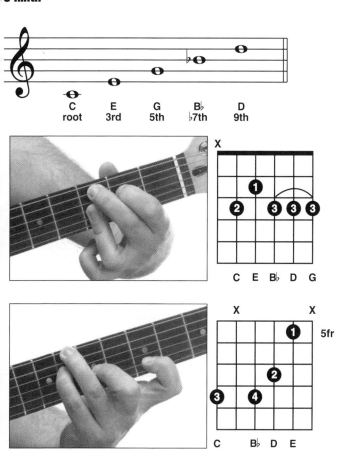

C E B♭ D G

5fr

C B♭ D E

C9sus4 (C9sus)
C ninth, suspended fourth

C	F	G	B♭	D
root	4th	5th	♭7th	9th

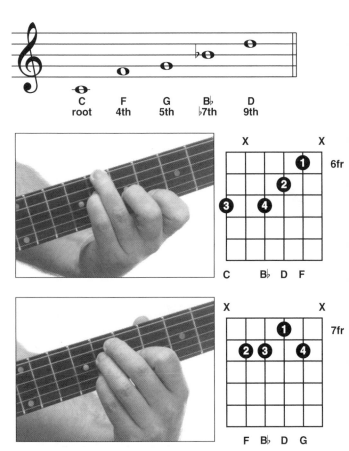

X · · · · X · · · · 6fr

C B♭ D F

X · · · · X · · · · 7fr

F B♭ D G

C7♭9 (C7-9, Cdom7♭9)
C dominant seventh, flat ninth

C	E	G	B♭	D♭
root	3rd	5th	♭7th	♭9th

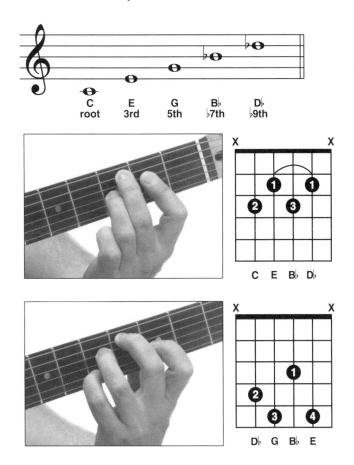

X · · · · X

C E B♭ D♭

X · · · · X

D♭ G B♭ E

C7#9 (C7+9, Cdom7#9)
C dominant seventh, sharp ninth

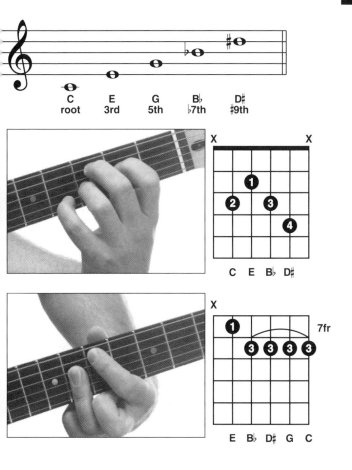

C	E	G	B♭	D#
root	3rd	5th	♭7th	#9th

C E B♭ D#

7fr

E B♭ D# G C

C7♭5(#9) (C7-5(+9), Cdom7♭5(#9))
C dominant seventh, flat fifth, sharp ninth

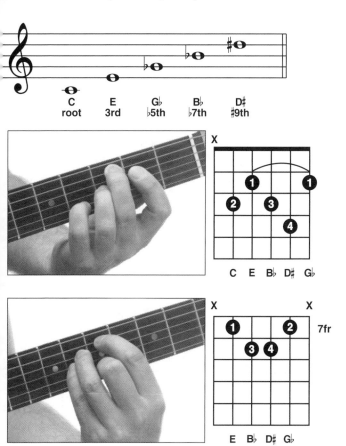

C	E	G♭	B♭	D#
root	3rd	♭5th	♭7th	#9th

C E B♭ D# G♭

C E B♭ D# G♭

7fr

E B♭ D# G♭

C11

C eleventh

C	E	G	B♭	D	F
root	3rd	5th	♭7th	9th	11th

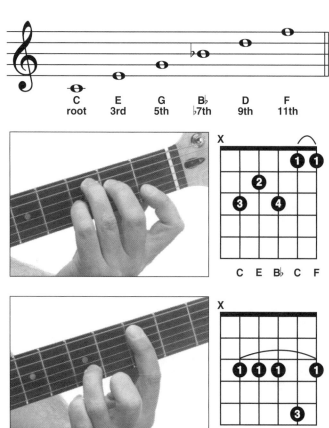

C E B♭ C F

C F B♭ E G

C7♯11 (C7+11, Cdom7♯11)

C dominant seventh, sharp eleventh

C	E	G	B♭	F♯
root	3rd	5th	♭7th	♯11th

B♭ E G C F♯

8fr

C F♯ B♭ E G C

C13 (Cdom13)
C thirteenth

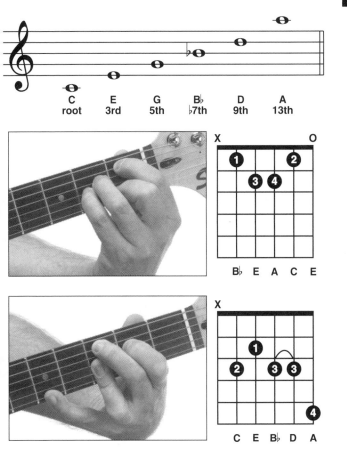

C	E	G	B♭	D	A
root	3rd	5th	♭7th	9th	13th

C13sus4 (C13sus)
C thirteenth, suspended fourth

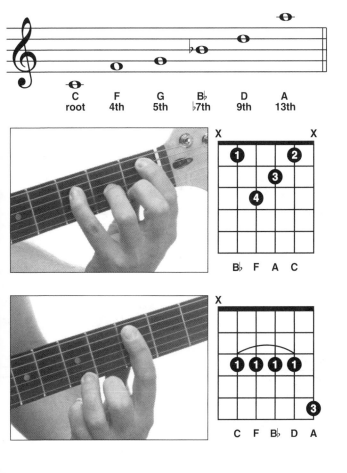

C	F	G	B♭	D	A
root	4th	5th	♭7th	9th	13th

C+ (Caug, C(♯5))
C augmented

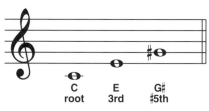

C — root
E — 3rd
G♯ — ♯5th

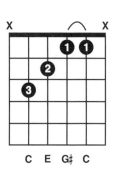

C E G♯ C

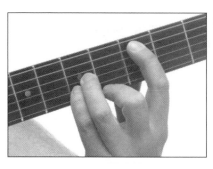

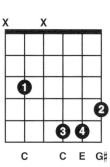

C   C E G♯

C+7 (C7♯5)
C dominant seventh, sharp fifth

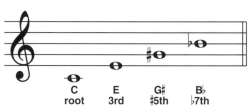

C — root
E — 3rd
G♯ — ♯5th
B♭ — ♭7th

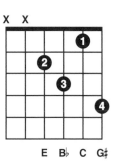

E B♭ C G♯

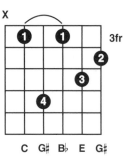

3fr

C G♯ B♭ E G♯

C° (C dim)
C diminished

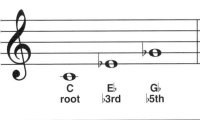

C	E♭	G♭
root	♭3rd	♭5th

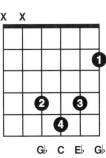

X X

①

② ③

④

G♭ C E♭ G♭

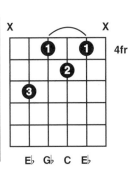

X X

① ① 4fr

②

③

E♭ G♭ C E♭

C°7 (Cdim7)
C diminished seventh

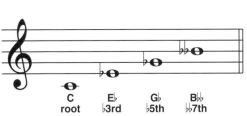

C	E♭	G♭	B♭♭
root	♭3rd	♭5th	♭♭7th

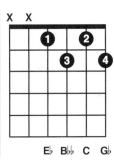

X X

① ②

③ ④

E♭ B♭♭ C G♭

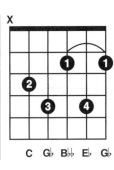

X

① ①

②

③ ④

C G♭ B♭♭ E♭ G♭

C# (C#maj)
C-sharp major

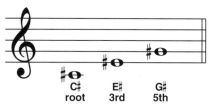

C# E# G#
root 3rd 5th

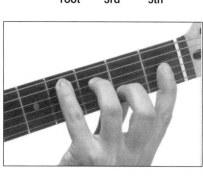

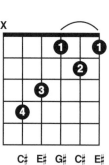

C# E# G# C# E#

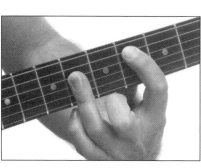

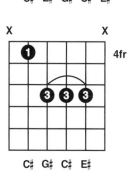

4fr

C# G# C# E#

C#5 (C# (no third))
C-sharp fifth (power chord)

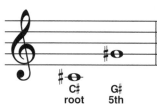

C# G#
root 5th

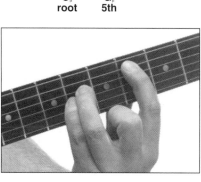

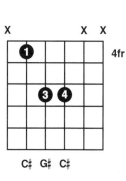

4fr

C# G# C#

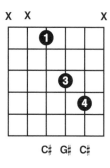

11fr

C# G# C#

C#sus4 (C#sus)
C-sharp suspended fourth

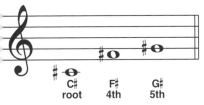

C#   F#   G#
root   4th   5th

X

① ①   ① 4fr
③
④

C# F# C# F# G#

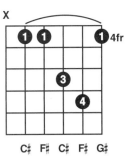

X X

① ①   6fr
②
④

G# C# F# C#

C#sus2 (C#5add2)
C-sharp suspended second

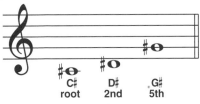

C#   D#   G#
root   2nd   5th

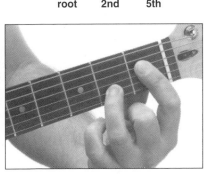

X X   X
① ①
③

D# G# C#

X
①   ① ① 4fr
③ ④

C# G# C# D# G#

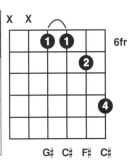
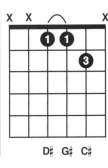
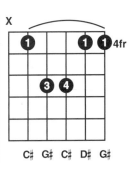

C#add9

C-sharp added ninth

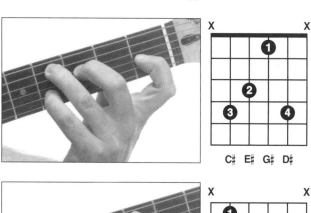

C#	E#	G#	D#
root	3rd	5th	9th

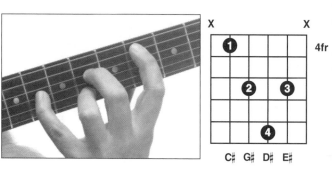

C#6

C-sharp sixth

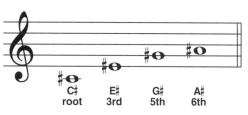

C#	E#	G#	A#
root	3rd	5th	6th

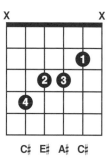

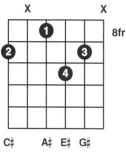

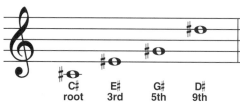

C#6/9 (C#6add9)
C-sharp sixth, added ninth

C#	E#	G#	A#	D#
root	3rd	5th	6th	9th

C# E# A# D# G#

C# D# G# C# E# A# — 6fr

C#maj7 (C#M7)
C-sharp major seventh

C#	E#	G#	B#
root	3rd	5th	7th

C# E# G# B# E#

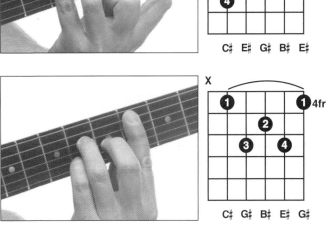

C# G# B# E# G# — 4fr

C#maj9 (C#M9)
C-sharp major ninth

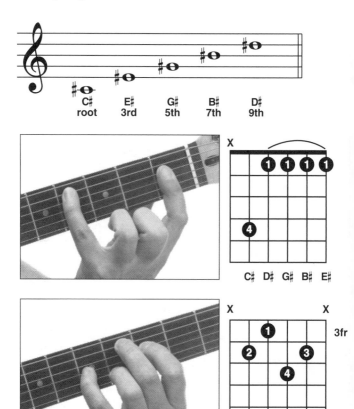

| C# | E# | G# | B# | D# |
| root | 3rd | 5th | 7th | 9th |

X

① ① ① ①

④

C# D# G# B# E#

X   X   3fr

①

② ③

④

C# E# B# D#

C#maj7#11 (C#M7#11)
C-sharp major seventh, sharp eleventh

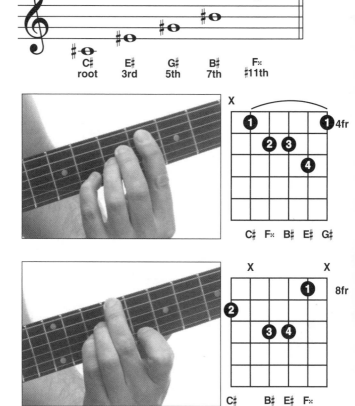

| C# | E# | G# | B# | F× |
| root | 3rd | 5th | 7th | #11th |

X

① ① 4fr

② ③

④

C# F× B# E# G#

X   X   8fr

①

②

③ ④

C# B# E# F×

C#maj13 (C#M13)

C-sharp major thirteenth

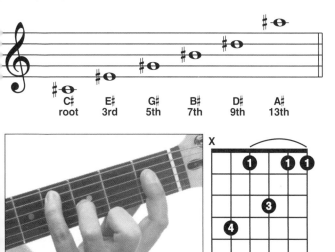

C#	E#	G#	B#	D#	A#
root	3rd	5th	7th	9th	13th

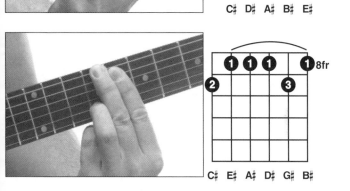

C# D# A# B# E#

8fr
C# E# A# D# G# B#

C#m (C#m, C#-)

C-sharp minor

C#	E	G#
root	♭3rd	5th

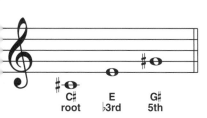

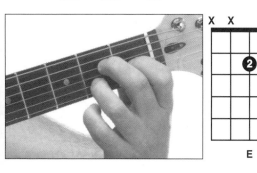

E G# C# E

4fr
C# G# C# E G#

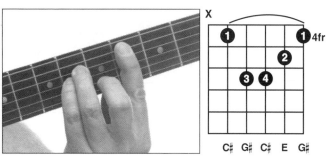

C#m(add9)

C-sharp minor, added ninth

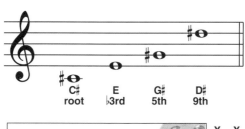

C#	E	G#	D#
root	♭3rd	5th	9th

X X   O

D# G# C# E

X   X   4fr

E G# C# D#

C#m6   (C#min6, C#-6)

C-sharp minor sixth

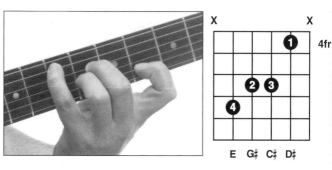

C#	E	G#	A#
root	♭3rd	5th	6th

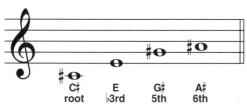

X

C# E A# C# G#

X   X   8fr

C# A# E G#

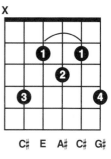

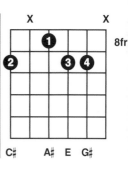

C#m♭6 (C#-(♭6), C#min♭6)
-sharp minor, flat sixth

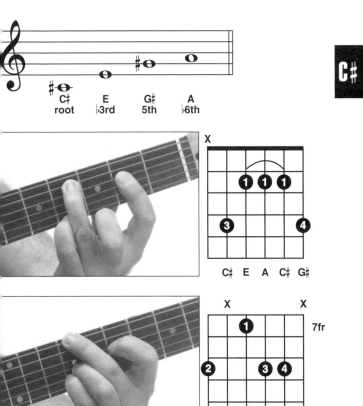

C#	E	G#	A
root	♭3rd	5th	♭6th

X

C# E A C# G#

X   X

7fr

C#   A   E   G#

C#m6/9
C-sharp minor sixth, added ninth

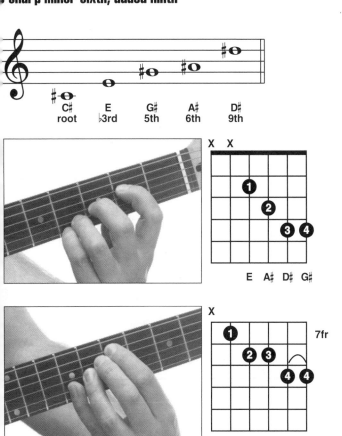

C#	E	G#	A#	D#
root	♭3rd	5th	6th	9th

X   X

E   A#   D#   G#

X

7fr

E   A#   D#   G#   C#

C#

C#m7 (C#min7, C#-7)
C-sharp minor seventh

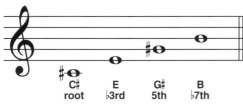

C# E G# B
root ♭3rd 5th ♭7th

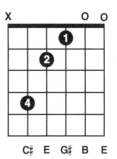

C# E G# B E

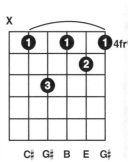

C# G# B E G#

C#m7♭5 (C#-7(♭5), C#min7-5)
C-sharp minor seventh, flat fifth

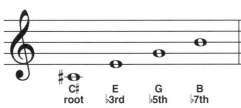

C# E G B
root ♭3rd ♭5th ♭7th

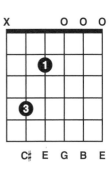

C# E G B E

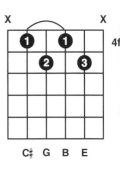

C# G B E

C#m(maj7) (C#m(+7))

C-sharp minor, major seventh

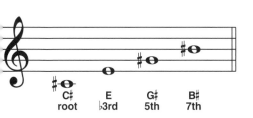

C#	E	G#	B#
root	♭3rd	5th	7th

C# E G# B#

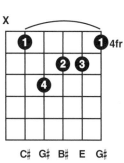

4fr

C# G# B# E G#

C#m9 (C#min9, C#-9)

C-sharp minor ninth

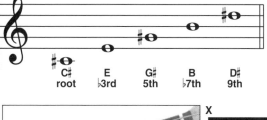

C#	E	G#	B	D#
root	♭3rd	5th	♭7th	9th

C# E B D#

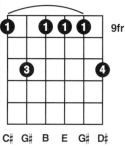

9fr

C# G# B E G# D#

C#m9♭5 (C#m9-5, C#min9♭5)
C-sharp minor ninth, flat fifth

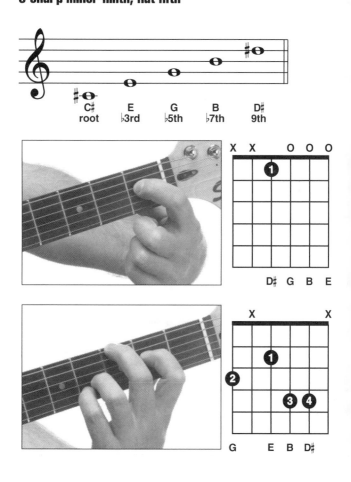

C#	E	G	B	D#
root	♭3rd	♭5th	♭7th	9th

C#m9(maj7) (C#m9+7, C#-9+7)
C-sharp minor ninth, major seventh

C#	E	G#	B#	D#
root	♭3rd	5th	7th	9th

C#m11 (C#-11, C#min11)

C-sharp minor eleventh

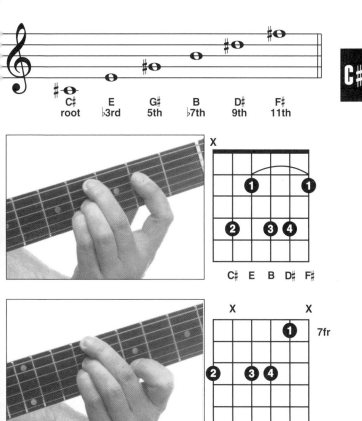

C#	E	G#	B	D#	F#
root	♭3rd	5th	♭7th	9th	11th

C# E B D# F#

C# B E F# 7fr

C#m13 (C#-13, C#min13)

C-sharp minor thirteenth

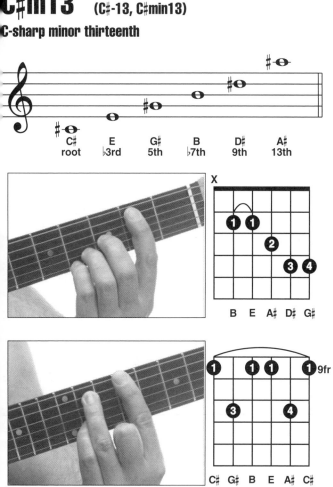

C#	E	G#	B	D#	A#
root	♭3rd	5th	♭7th	9th	13th

B E A# D# G#

C# G# B E A# C# 9fr

C#7 (C#dom7)
C-sharp dominant seventh

C#   E#   G#   B
root   3rd   5th   ♭7th

C# E# B C#

C# G# B E# G# C#   9fr

C#7sus4 (C#7sus)
C-sharp dominant seventh, suspended fourth

C#   F#   G#   B
root   4th   5th   ♭7th

C# F# B C#

C# G# B F# G# C#   9fr

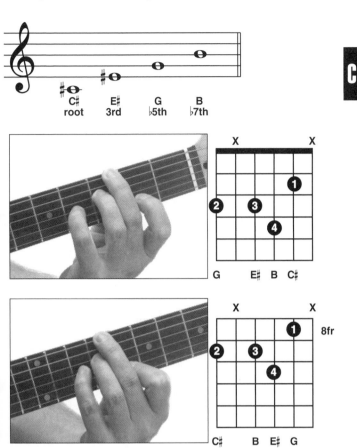

C#7♭5 (C#7-5, C#dom7♭5)

C-sharp dominant seventh, flat fifth

C#	E#	G	B
root	3rd	♭5th	♭7th

C#

X   X

② ③ ④ ①

G   E# B   C#

X   X   8fr

② ③ ④ ①

C#   B   E# G

C#9

C-sharp ninth

C#	E#	G#	B	D#
root	3rd	5th	♭7th	9th

X

① ② ③ ③ ③

C# E# B   D# G#

X   X   6fr

① ② ③ ④

C#   B   D# E#

C#9sus4 (C#9sus)
C-sharp ninth, suspended fourth

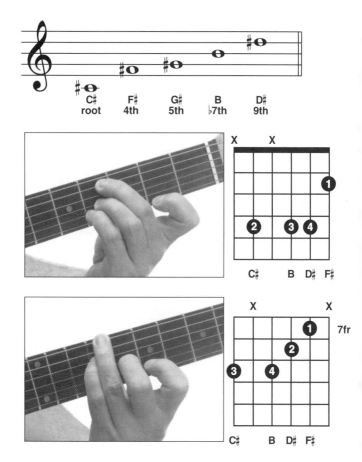

C#	F#	G#	B	D#
root	4th	5th	♭7th	9th

C#7♭9 (C#7-9, C#dom7♭9)
C-sharp dominant seventh, flat ninth

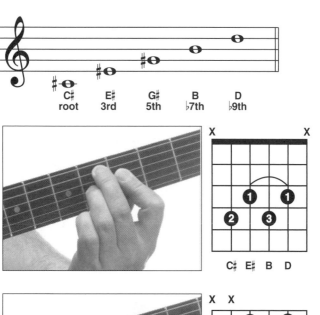

C#	E#	G#	B	D
root	3rd	5th	♭7th	♭9th

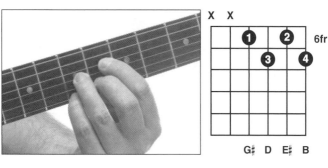

C#7#9 (C#7+9, C#dom7#9)
C-sharp dominant seventh, sharp ninth

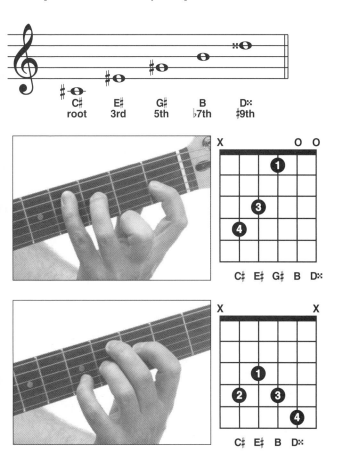

C#	E#	G#	B	D𝄪
root	3rd	5th	♭7th	#9th

C#7♭5(#9) (C#7-5(+9), C#dom7♭5(#9))
C-sharp dominant seventh, flat fifth, sharp ninth

C#	E#	G	B	D𝄪
root	3rd	♭5th	♭7th	#9th

C#11
C-sharp eleventh

C#	E#	G#	B	D#	F#
root	3rd	5th	♭7th	9th	11th

X

C# E# B C# F#

X 4fr

C# F# B E# G#

C#7#11 (C#7+11, C#dom7#11)
C-sharp dominant seventh, sharp eleventh

C#	E#	G#	B	F×
root	3rd	5th	♭7th	#11th

X   O O

C# E# F× B G#

X   6fr

E# G# C# F× B

C#13 (C#dom13)
C-sharp thirteenth

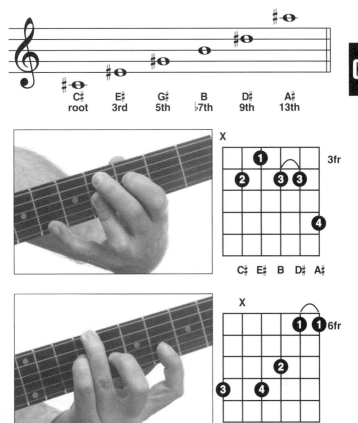

C#	E#	G#	B	D#	A#
root	3rd	5th	♭7th	9th	13th

C#13sus4 (C#13sus)
C-sharp thirteenth, suspended fourth

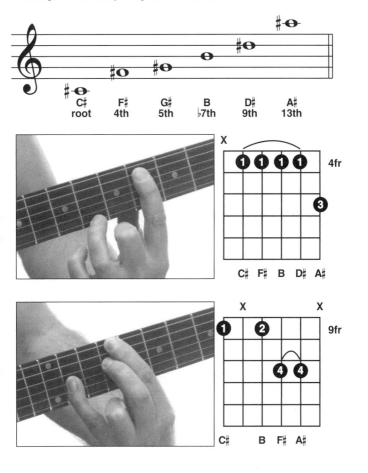

C#	F#	G#	B	D#	A#
root	4th	5th	♭7th	9th	13th

C#+ (C#aug, C#(#5))
C-sharp augmented

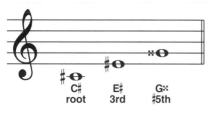

C# — root
E# — 3rd
G𝄪 — #5th

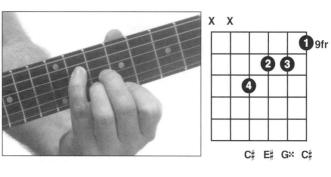

X   X

C# E# G𝄪 C#

X X

9fr

C# E# G𝄪 C#

C#+7 (C#7#5)
C-sharp dominant seventh, sharp fifth

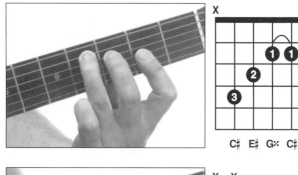

C# — root
E# — 3rd
G𝄪 — #5th
B — ♭7th

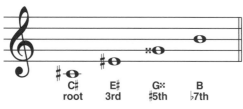

X   O

C# E# G𝄪 B E#

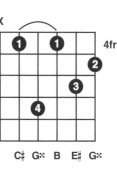

X

4fr

C# G𝄪 B E# G𝄪

C#° (C#dim)
C-sharp diminished

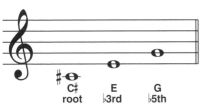

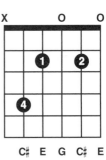

C# E G C# E

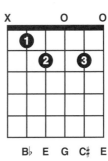

G C# E G

C#°7 (C#dim7)
C-sharp diminished seventh

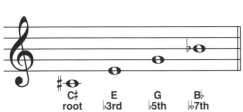

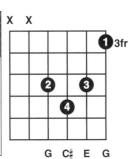

Bb E G C# E

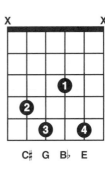

C# G Bb E

D (Dmaj)
D major

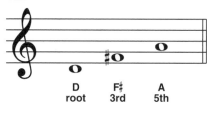

D   F#   A
root 3rd   5th

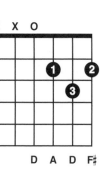

X X O

① | ②
③

D A D F#

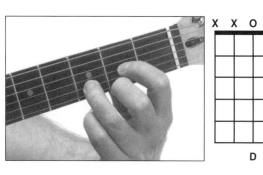

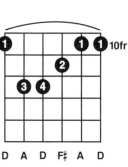

① | ① ① 10fr
②
③ ④

D A D F# A D

D5 (D (no 3rd))
D fifth (power chord)

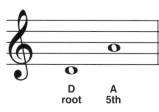

D   A
root 5th

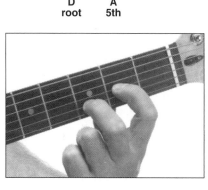

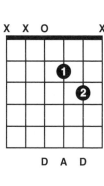

X X O   X

①
②

D A D

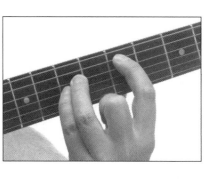

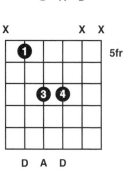

X   X X

①   5fr

③ ④

D A D

Dsus4 (Dsus)

D suspended fourth

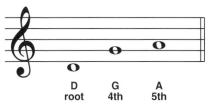

D	G	A
root	4th	5th

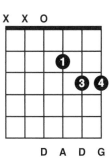

X X O

D A D G

1 1 ... 1 1 10fr

D G D G A D

Dsus2 (D5add2)

D suspended second

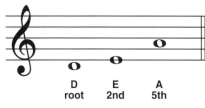

D	E	A
root	2nd	5th

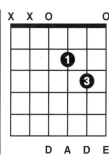

X X O O

D A D E

X X 9fr

D E A E

Dadd9
D added ninth

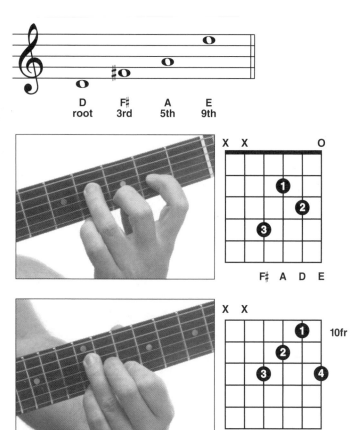

D	F#	A	E
root	3rd	5th	9th

F# A D E

X X — — — O

X X — — —   10fr

D F# A E

D6
D sixth

D	F#	A	B
root	3rd	5th	6th

X X O — O

D A B F#

X — — — X   9fr

D B F# A

D6/9 (D6add9)

D sixth, added ninth

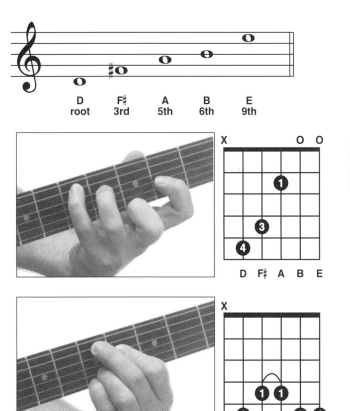

D	F#	A	B	E
root	3rd	5th	6th	9th

X   O O

D F# A B E

X

D F# B E A

Dmaj7 (DM7)

D major seventh

D	F#	A	C#
root	3rd	5th	7th

X X O

D A C# F#

X   X   10fr

D C# F# A

Dmaj9 (DM9)

D major ninth

D	F#	A	C#	E
root	3rd	5th	7th	9th

Dmaj7♯11 (DM7♯11)

D major seventh, sharp eleventh

D	F#	A	C#	G#
root	3rd	5th	7th	♯11th

Dmaj13 (DM13)

D major thirteenth

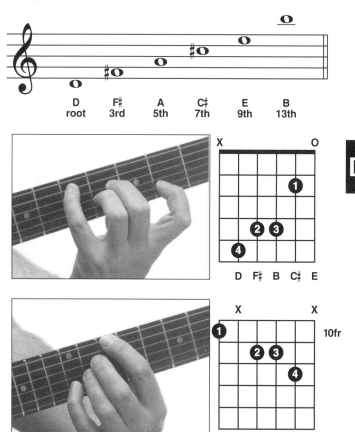

D	F#	A	C#	E	B
root	3rd	5th	7th	9th	13th

X   O

D   F#   B   C#   E

X   X   10fr

D   C#   F#   B

Dm (Dmin, D-)

D minor

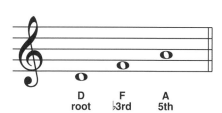

D	F	A
root	b3rd	5th

X   X   O

D   A   D   F

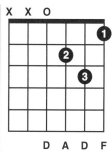

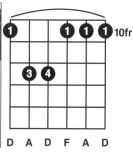

10fr

D   A   D   F   A   D

Dm(add9)

D minor, added ninth

D root	F ♭3rd	A 5th	E 9th

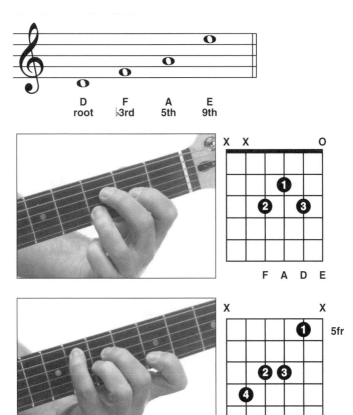

X X   O

F   A   D   E

X   X   5fr

F   A   D   E

Dm6 (Dmin6, D-6)

D minor sixth

D root	F ♭3rd	A 5th	B 6th

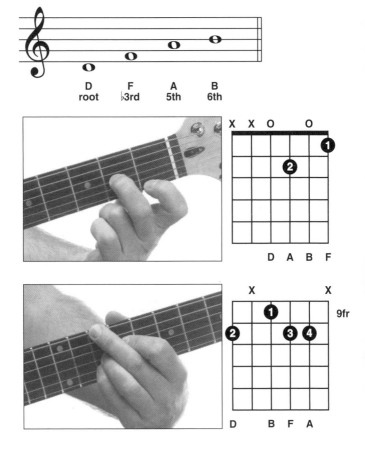

X X O   O

D   A   B   F

X   X   9fr

D   B   F   A

Dm♭6 (D-(♭6), Dmin♭6)

D minor, flat sixth

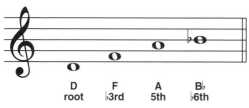

D	F	A	B♭
root	♭3rd	5th	♭6th

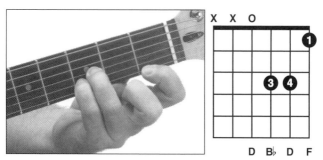

X X O

D B♭ D F

X

5fr

D A D F B♭

Dm6/9

D minor sixth, added ninth

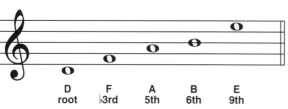

D	F	A	B	E
root	♭3rd	5th	6th	9th

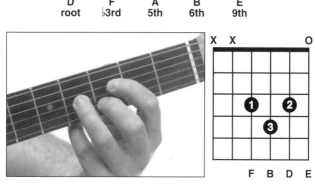

X X O

F B D E

X X

10fr

D F B E

D

Dm7 (D-7, Dmin7)
D minor seventh

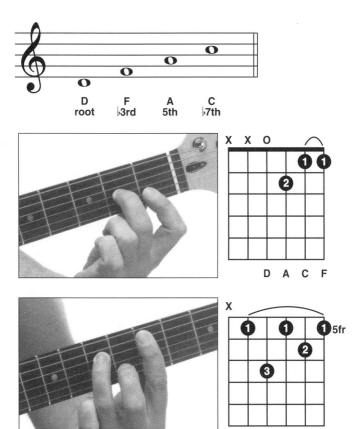

D   F   A   C
root   ♭3rd   5th   ♭7th

Dm7♭5 (D-7♭5, Dmin7-5)
D minor seventh, flat fifth

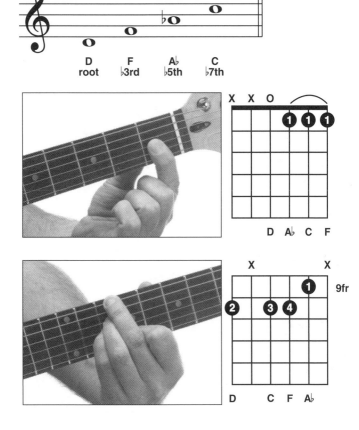

D   F   A♭   C
root   ♭3rd   ♭5th   ♭7th

Dm(maj7) (D-(+7))

D minor, major seventh

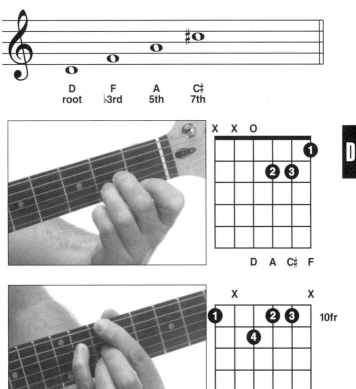

D	F	A	C#
root	♭3rd	5th	7th

D A C# F

10fr

D C# F A

Dm9 (D-9, Dmin9)

D minor ninth

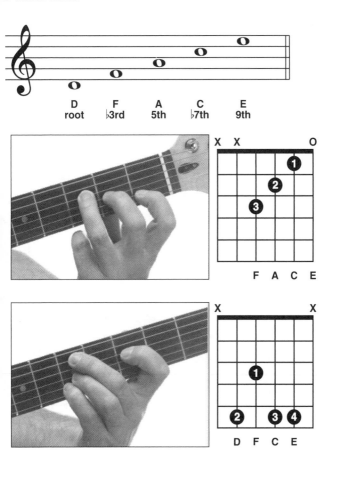

D	F	A	C	E
root	♭3rd	5th	♭7th	9th

F A C E

D F C E

Dm9♭5 (Dm9-5, Dmin9♭5)

D minor ninth, flat fifth

D	F	A♭	C	E
root	♭3rd	♭5th	♭7th	9th

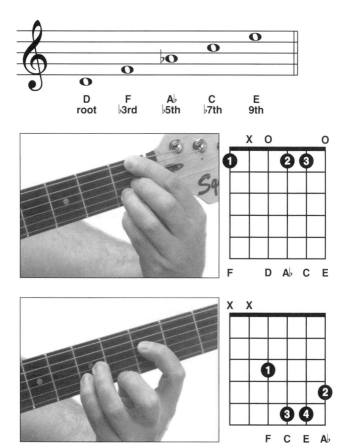

Dm9(maj7) (Dm9+7, D-9+7)

D minor ninth, major seventh

D	F	A	C#	E
root	♭3rd	5th	7th	9th

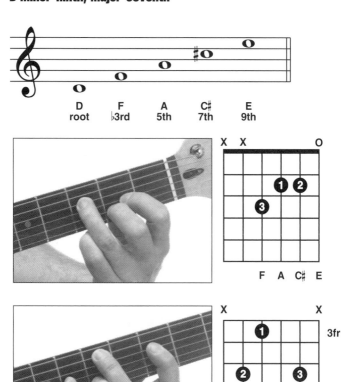

Dm11 (D-11, Dmin11)
D minor eleventh

D	F	A	C	E	G
root	♭3rd	5th	♭7th	9th	11th

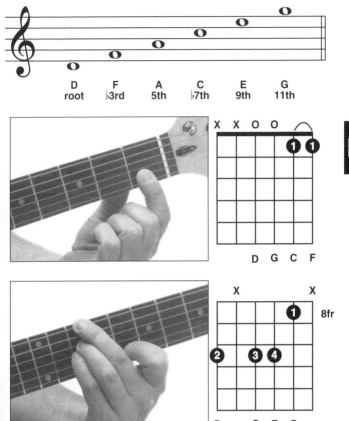

Dm13 (D-13, Dmin13)
D minor thirteenth

D	F	A	C	E	B
root	♭3rd	5th	♭7th	9th	13th

D7 (Ddom7)
D dominant seventh

D	F♯	A	C
root	3rd	5th	♭7th

D7sus4 (D7sus)
D dominant seventh, suspended fourth

D	G	A	C
root	4th	5th	♭7th

D7♭5 (D7-5, Ddom7♭5)

dominant seventh, flat fifth

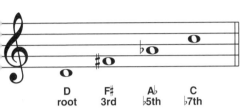

D	F♯	A♭	C
root	3rd	♭5th	♭7th

D

D A♭ C F♯

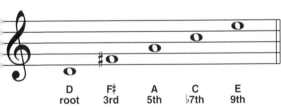

F♯ C D A♭

D9

D ninth

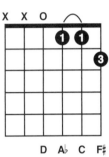

D	F♯	A	C	E
root	3rd	5th	♭7th	9th

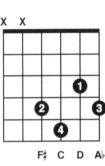

F♯ A C E

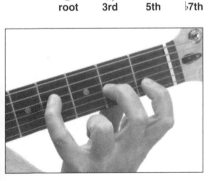

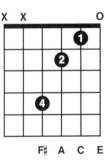

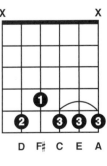

D F♯ C E A

D9sus4 (D9sus)

D ninth, suspended fourth

D	G	A	C	E
root	4th	5th	♭7th	9th

X O O O   O

A D G C E

X

7fr

E A D G C

D7♭9 (D7-9, Ddom7♭9)

D dominant seventh, flat ninth

D	F♯	A	C	E♭
root	3rd	5th	♭7th	♭9th

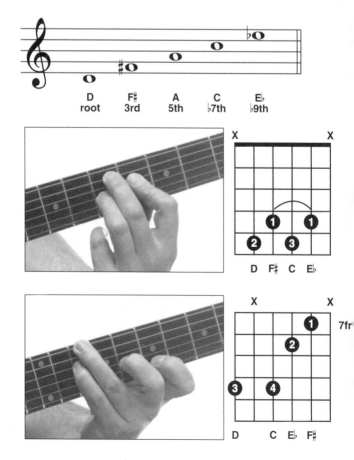

X   X

D F♯ C E♭

X   X

7fr

D   C E♭ F♯

7#9 (D7+9, Ddom7#9)

dominant seventh, sharp ninth

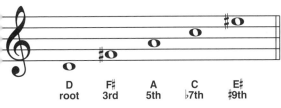

D	F#	A	C	E#
root	3rd	5th	♭7th	#9th

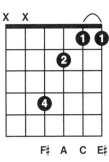

F# A C E#

F# C E# A D

7♭5(#9) (D7-5(+9), Ddom7♭5(#9))

dominant seventh, flat fifth, sharp ninth

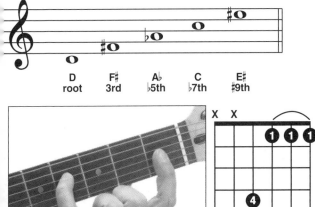

D	F#	A♭	C	E#
root	3rd	♭5th	♭7th	#9th

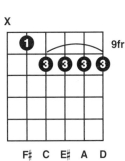

F# A♭ C E#

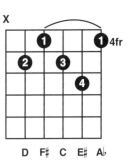

D F# C E# A♭

D

D11

D eleventh

D	F#	A	C	E	G
root	3rd	5th	♭7th	9th	11th

X X O O

D G C F#

X

D F# C D G

D7♯11 (D7+11, Ddom7♯11)

D dominant seventh, sharp eleventh

D	F#	A	C	G#
root	3rd	5th	♭7th	♯11th

X X O

D G# C F#

5fr

A D G# C F# A

D13 (Ddom13)

D thirteenth

D root	F# 3rd	A 5th	C ♭7th	E 9th	B 13th

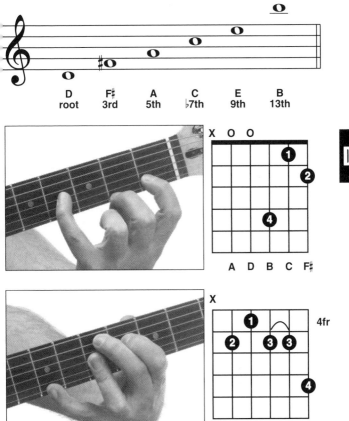

X O O

A D B C F#

X

4fr

D F# C E B

D13sus4 (D13sus)

D thirteenth, suspended fourth

D root	G 4th	A 5th	C ♭7th	E 9th	B 13th

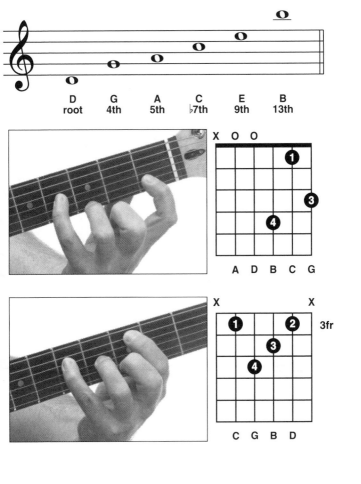

X O O

A D B C G

X X

3fr

C G B D

D

D+ (Daug, D(#5))
D augmented

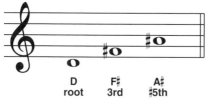

D	F#	A#
root	3rd	#5th

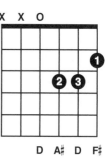

X X O

D A# D F#

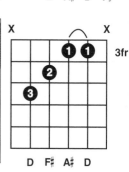

X   X   3fr

D F# A# D

D+7 (D7#5)
D dominant seventh, sharp fifth

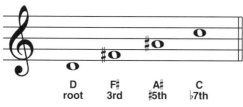

D	F#	A#	C
root	3rd	#5th	b7th

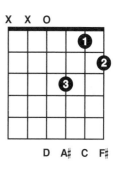

X X O

D A# C F#

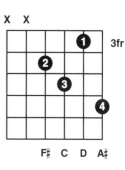

X X   3fr

F# C D A#

D° (D dim)
diminished

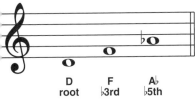

D	F	A♭
root	♭3rd	♭5th

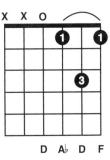

X X O ⌢

D A♭ D F

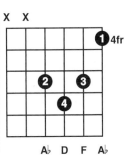

X X   4fr

A♭ D F A♭

D

D°7 (Ddim7)
diminished seventh

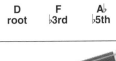

D	F	A♭	C♭
root	♭3rd	♭5th	♭♭7th

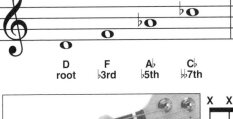
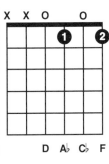

X X O   O

D A♭ C♭ F

X   4fr

D A♭ C♭ F A♭

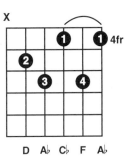

E♭ (E♭maj)
E-flat major

E♭	G	B♭
root	3rd	5th

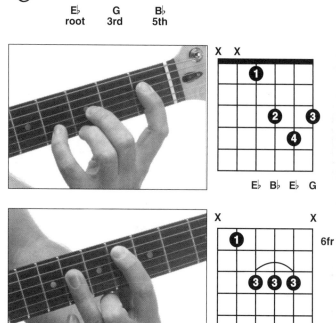

X X

E♭ B♭ E♭ G

X X

6fr

E♭ B♭ E♭ G

E♭5 (E♭(no3))
E-flat fifth (power chord)

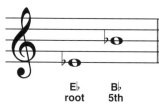

E♭	B♭
root	5th

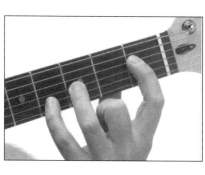

X X X

E♭ B♭ E♭

X X X

6fr

E♭ B♭ E♭

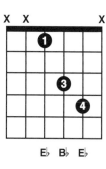

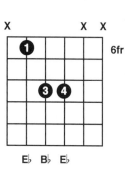

E♭ sus4 (E♭sus)

E-flat suspended fourth

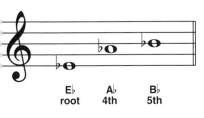

E♭   A♭   B♭
root   4th   5th

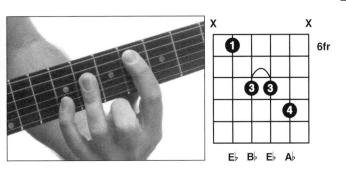

A♭   E♭   B♭   E♭

E♭

6fr

E♭   B♭   E♭   A♭

E♭ sus2 (E♭5add2)

E-flat suspended second

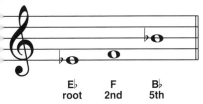

E♭   F   B♭
root   2nd   5th

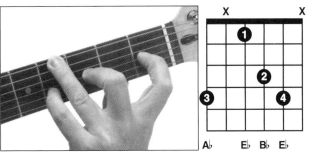

E♭   B♭   E♭   F

6fr

E♭   B♭   E♭   F   B♭

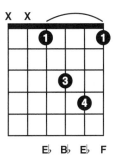

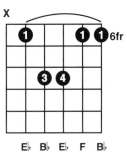

E♭add9
E-flat added ninth

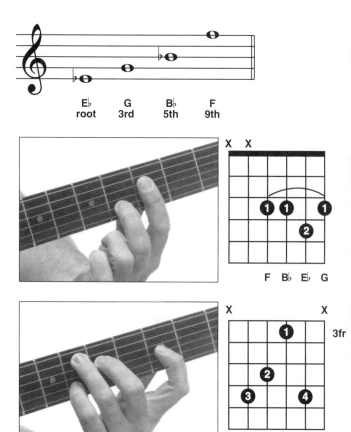

E♭	G	B♭	F
root	3rd	5th	9th

F B♭ E♭ G

3fr

E♭ G B♭ F

E♭6
E-flat sixth

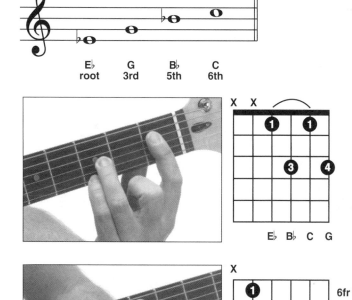

E♭	G	B♭	C
root	3rd	5th	6th

E♭ B♭ C G

6fr

E♭ B♭ E♭ G C

E♭6/9 (E♭6add9)

E-flat sixth, added ninth

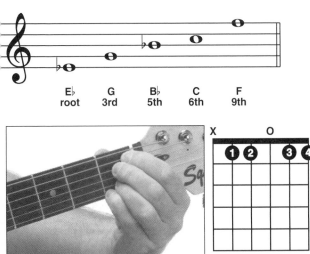

E♭	G	B♭	C	F
root	3rd	5th	6th	9th

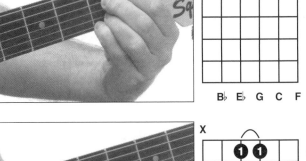

B♭ E♭ G C F

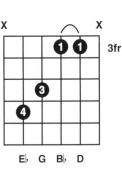
E♭

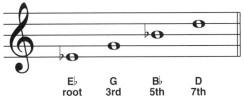

5fr

E♭ G C F B♭

E♭maj7 (E♭M7)

E-flat major seventh

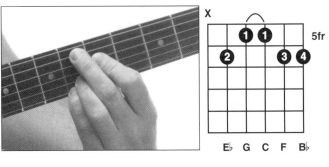

E♭	G	B♭	D
root	3rd	5th	7th

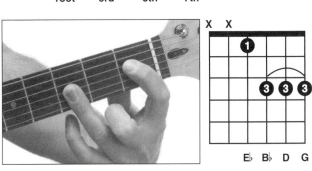

E♭ B♭ D G

3fr

E♭ G B♭ D

E♭maj9 (E♭M9)

E-flat major ninth

E♭	G	B♭	D	F
root	3rd	5th	7th	9th

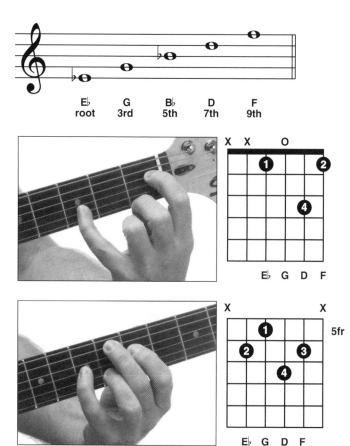

E♭ G D F

E♭ G D F   5fr

E♭maj7♯11 (E♭M7♯11)

E-flat major seventh, sharp eleventh

E♭	G	B♭	D	A
root	3rd	5th	7th	♯11th

E♭ A D G

E♭ A D G   6fr

E♭maj13 (E♭M13)

E-flat major thirteenth

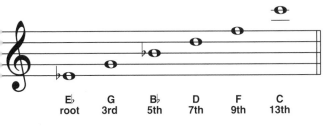

E♭	G	B♭	D	F	C
root	3rd	5th	7th	9th	13th

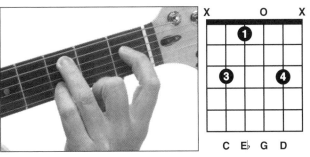

C E♭ G D

E♭ G D G C

5fr

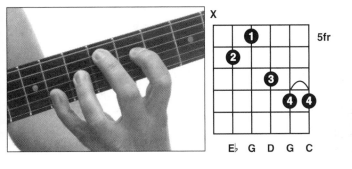

E♭m (E♭min, E♭-)

E-flat minor

E♭	G♭	B♭
root	♭3rd	5th

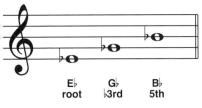

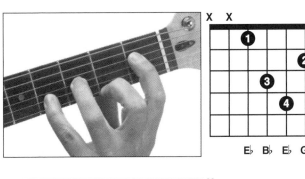

E♭ B♭ E♭ G♭

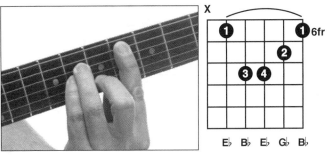

E♭ B♭ E♭ G♭ B♭

6fr

E♭m(add9)

E-flat minor, added ninth

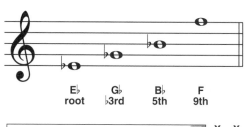

E♭	G♭	B♭	F
root	♭3rd	5th	9th

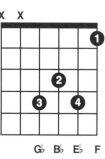

G♭ B♭ E♭ F

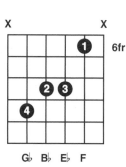

6fr

G♭ B♭ E♭ F

E♭m6 (E♭min6, E♭-6)

E-flat minor sixth

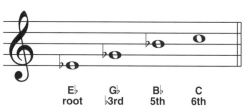

E♭	G♭	B♭	C
root	♭3rd	5th	6th

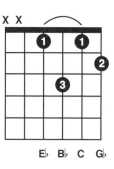

E♭ B♭ C G♭

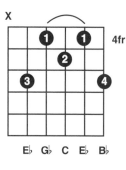

4fr

E♭ G♭ C E♭ B♭

E♭m♭6 (E♭-(♭6), E♭min ♭6)

E-flat minor, flat sixth

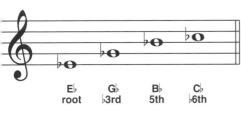

E♭	G♭	B♭	C♭
root	♭3rd	5th	♭6th

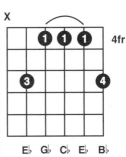

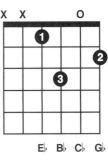

X X   O

E♭ B♭ C♭ G♭

X

4fr

E♭ G♭ C♭ E♭ B♭

E♭m6/9

E-flat minor sixth, added ninth

E♭	G♭	B♭	C	F
root	♭3rd	5th	6th	9th

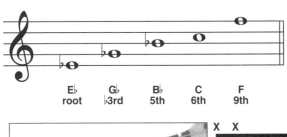

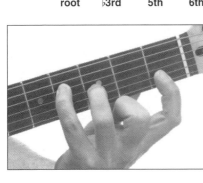

X X

G♭ B♭ C F

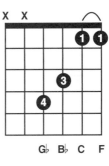

X   X

4fr

E♭ G♭ C F

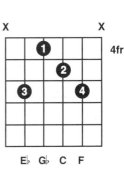

E♭m7 (E♭min7, E♭-7)

E-flat minor seventh

E♭	G♭	B♭	D♭
root	♭3rd	5th	♭7th

X X

E♭ B♭ D♭ G♭

X X

11fr

E♭ D♭ G♭ B♭

E♭m7♭5 (E♭-7♭5, E♭min7-5)

E-flat minor seventh, flat fifth

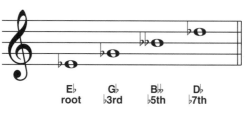

E♭	G♭	B♭♭	D♭
root	♭3rd	♭5th	♭7th

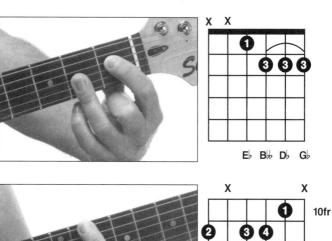

X X

E♭ B♭♭ D♭ G♭

X X

10fr

E♭ D♭ G♭ B♭♭

E♭m(maj7) (E♭-(+7))

E-flat minor, major seventh

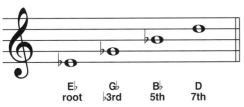

E♭	G♭	B♭	D
root	♭3rd	5th	7th

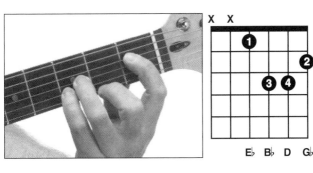

E♭ B♭ D G♭

E♭

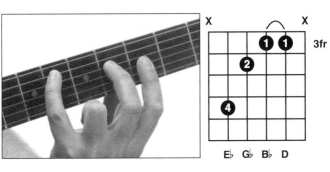

3fr

E♭ G♭ B♭ D

E♭m9 (E♭min9, E♭-9)

E-flat minor ninth

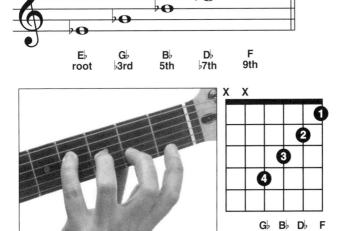

E♭	G♭	B♭	D♭	F
root	♭3rd	5th	♭7th	9th

G♭ B♭ D♭ F

4fr

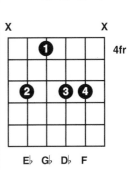

E♭ G♭ D♭ F

E♭m9♭5 (E♭m9-5, E♭min9♭5)
E-flat minor ninth, flat fifth

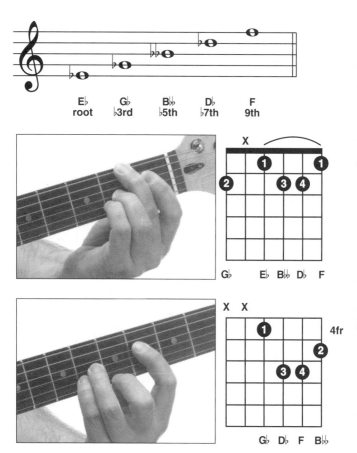

E♭	G♭	B♭♭	D♭	F
root	♭3rd	♭5th	♭7th	9th

E♭m9(maj7) (E♭m9+7, E♭-9+7)
E-flat minor ninth, major seventh

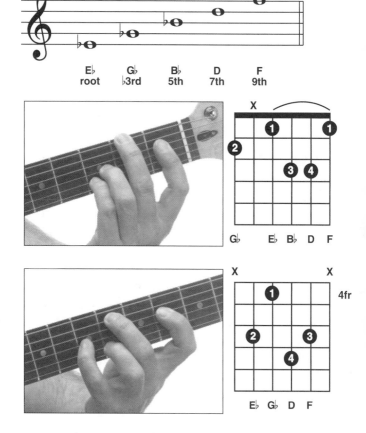

E♭	G♭	B♭	D	F
root	♭3rd	5th	7th	9th

E♭m11 (E♭-11, E♭min11)

E-flat minor eleventh

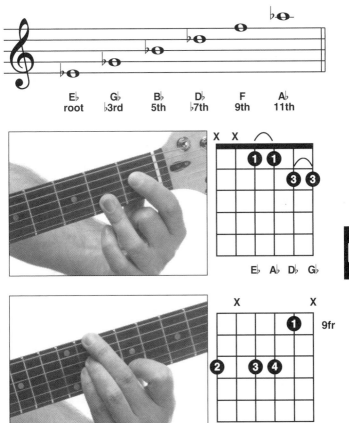

E♭	G♭	B♭	D♭	F	A♭
root	♭3rd	5th	♭7th	9th	11th

E♭ A♭ D♭ G♭

E♭ D♭ G♭ A♭

9fr

E♭

E♭m13 (E♭-13, E♭min13)

E-flat minor thirteenth

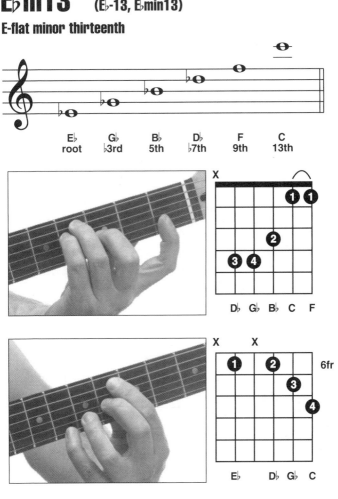

E♭	G♭	B♭	D♭	F	C
root	♭3rd	5th	♭7th	9th	13th

D♭ G♭ B♭ C F

E♭ D♭ G♭ C

6fr

E♭7 (E♭dom7)
E-flat dominant seventh

E♭   G   B♭   D♭
root   3rd   5th   ♭7th

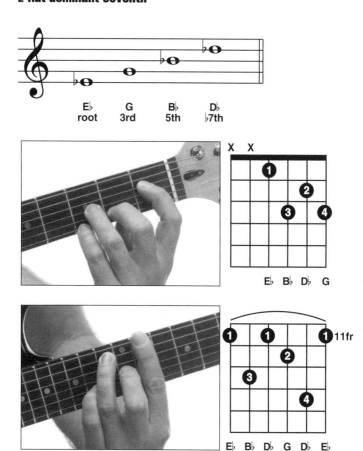

E♭   B♭   D♭   G

11fr

E♭   B♭   D♭   G   D♭   E♭

E♭7sus4 (E♭7sus)
E-flat dominant seventh, suspended fourth

E♭   A♭   B♭   D♭
root   4th   5th   ♭7th

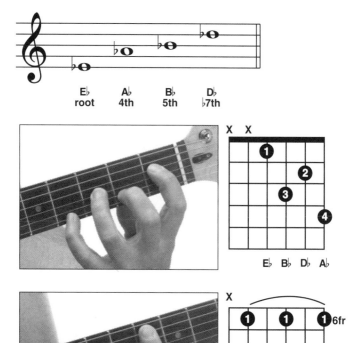

E♭   B♭   D♭   A♭

6fr

E♭   B♭   D♭   A♭   B♭

E♭7♭5 (E♭7-5, E♭dom7♭5)
E-flat dominant seventh, flat fifth

E♭	G	B♭♭	D♭
root	3rd	♭5th	♭7th

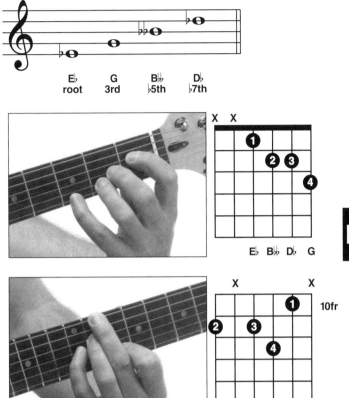

E♭9
E-flat ninth

E♭	G	B♭	D♭	F
root	3rd	5th	♭7th	9th

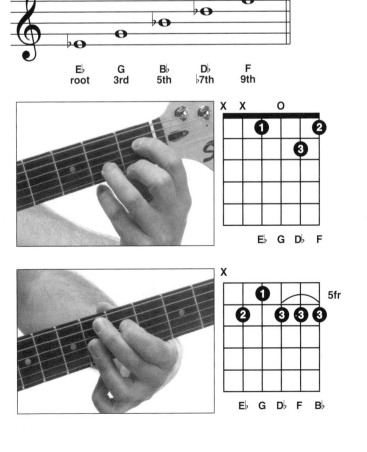

E♭9sus4 (E♭9sus)

E-flat ninth, suspended fourth

E♭	A♭	B♭	D♭	F
root	4th	5th	♭7th	9th

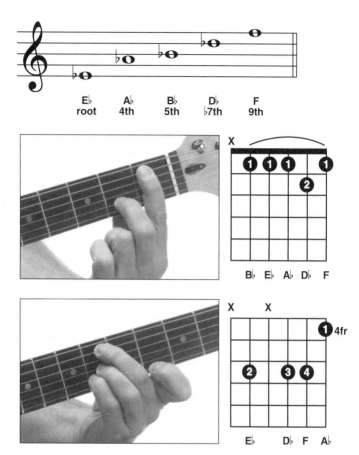

B♭ E♭ A♭ D♭ F

E♭ D♭ F A♭

E♭7♭9 (E♭7-9, E♭dom7♭9)

E-flat dominant seventh, flat ninth

E♭	G	B♭	D♭	F♭
root	3rd	5th	♭7th	♭9th

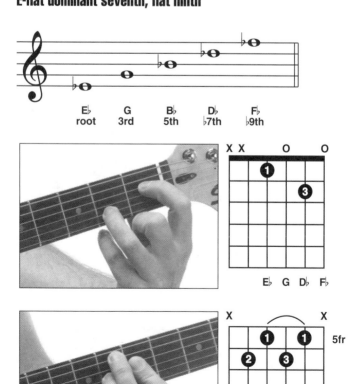

E♭ G D♭ F♭

E♭ G D♭ F♭

E♭7♯9 (E♭7+9, E♭dom7♯9)

E-flat dominant seventh, sharp ninth

E♭	G	B♭	D♭	F♯
root	3rd	5th	♭7th	♯9th

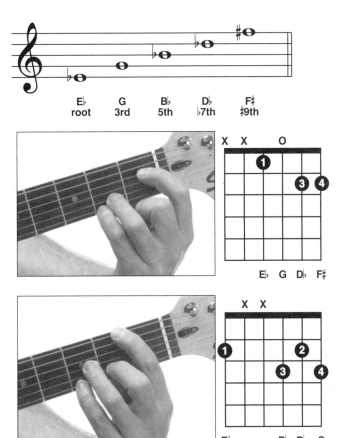

E♭ G D♭ F♯

F♯ B♭ D♭ G

Eb

E♭7♭5(♯9) (E♭7-5(+9), E♭dom7♭5(♯9))

E-flat dominant seventh, flat fifth, sharp ninth

E♭	G	B♭♭	D♭	F♯
root	3rd	♭5th	♭7th	♯9th

B♭♭ E♭ G D♭ F♯

E♭ G D♭ F♯ B♭♭

E♭11
E-flat eleventh

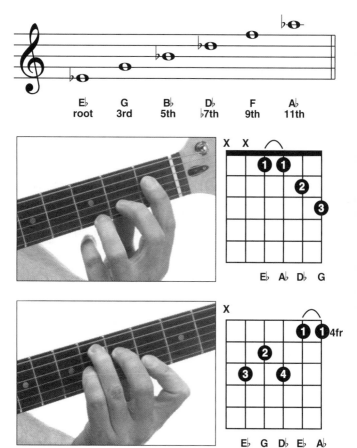

E♭	G	B♭	D♭	F	A♭
root	3rd	5th	♭7th	9th	11th

E♭7♯11 (E♭7+11, E♭dom7♯11)
E-flat dominant seventh, sharp eleventh

E♭	G	B♭	D♭	A
root	3rd	5th	♭7th	♯11th

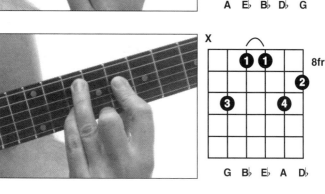

E♭13 (E♭dom13)
E-flat dominant thirteenth

E♭	G	B♭	D♭	F	C
root	3rd	5th	♭7th	9th	13th

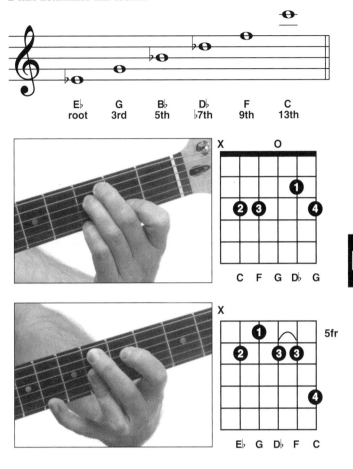

Eb

E♭13sus4 (E♭13sus)
E-flat thirteenth, suspended fourth

E♭	A♭	B♭	D♭	F	C
root	4th	5th	♭7th	9th	13th

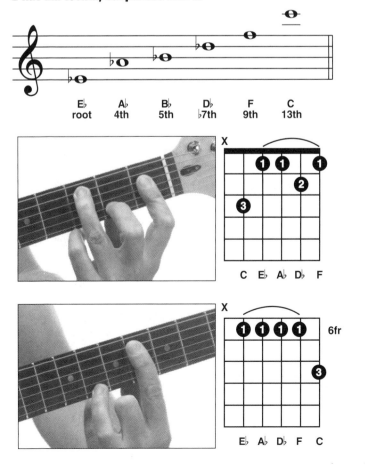

E♭+ (E♭aug, E♭(♯5))
E-flat augmented

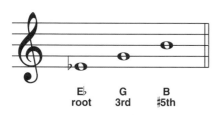

E♭	G	B
root	3rd	♯5th

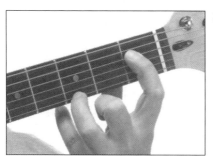
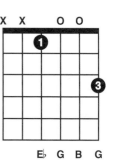

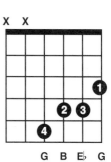

E♭+7 (E♭7♯5)
E-flat dominant seventh, sharp fifth

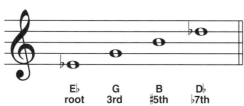

E♭	G	B	D♭
root	3rd	♯5th	♭7th

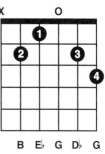

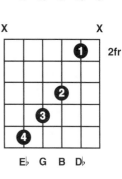

E♭° (E♭dim)
E-flat diminished

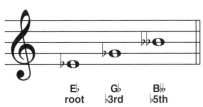

E♭	G♭	B♭♭
root	♭3rd	♭5th

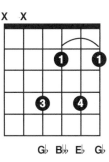

X X

① ①
③ ④

G♭ B♭ E♭ G♭

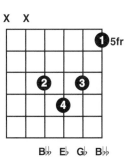

X X

①5fr
② ③
④

B♭♭ E♭ G♭ B♭♭

E♭

E♭°7 (E♭dim7)
E-flat diminished seventh

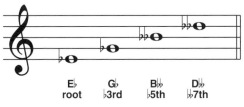

E♭	G♭	B♭♭	D♭♭
root	♭3rd	♭5th	♭7th

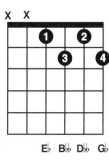

X X

① ②
③ ④

E♭ B♭♭ D♭♭ G♭

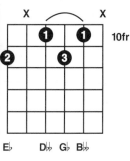

X X

① ①
② ③

10fr

E♭ D♭♭ G♭ B♭♭

E (Emaj)
E major

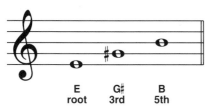

E — root
G# — 3rd
B — 5th

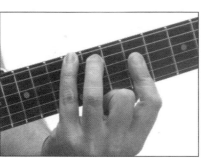
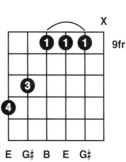

E B E G# B E

E G# B E G#

E5 (E(no3rd))
E fifth (power chord)

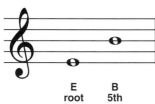

E — root
B — 5th

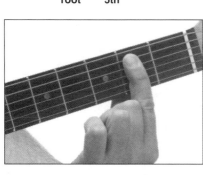
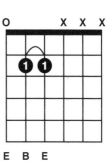

E B E

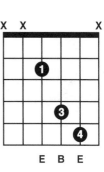

E B E

Esus4 (Esus)
E suspended fourth

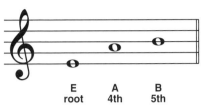

E	A	B
root	4th	5th

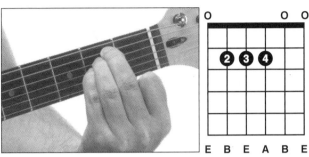

O   O   O

② ③ ④

E B E A B E

X X

①

③

④ ④

E B E A

Esus2 (E5add2)
E suspended second

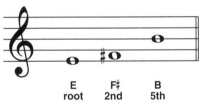

E	F♯	B
root	2nd	5th

X X

①   ①

③

④

E B E F♯

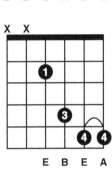

X X

① ①

②

④

4fr

F♯ B E B

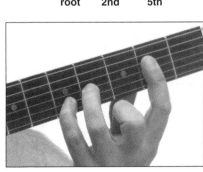

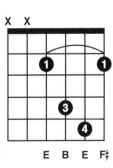

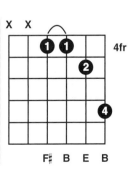

E

Eadd9

E added ninth

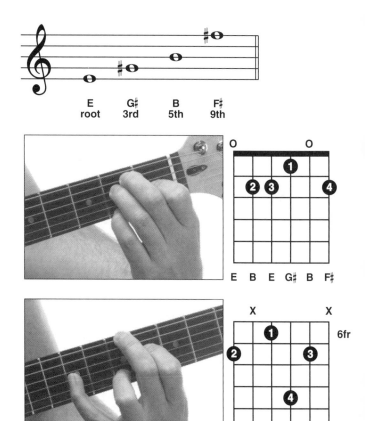

E	G#	B	F#
root	3rd	5th	9th

O · · 1 · O
2 3 · 4

E B E G# B F#

X · 1 · X 6fr
2 · 3
4

B G# E F#

E6

E sixth

E	G#	B	C#
root	3rd	5th	6th

O · 1 · O
2 3 · 4

E B E G# C# E

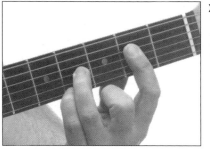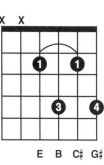

X X
1 · 1
3 4

E B C# G#

E6/9 (E6add9)
E sixth, added ninth

E	G#	B	C#	F#
root	3rd	5th	6th	9th

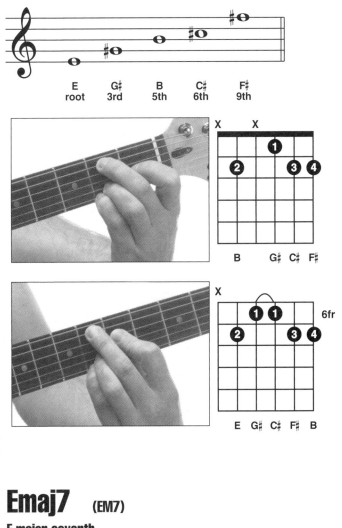

X   X

B   G# C# F#

X

6fr

E G# C# F# B

E

Emaj7 (EM7)
E major seventh

E	G#	B	D#
root	3rd	5th	7th

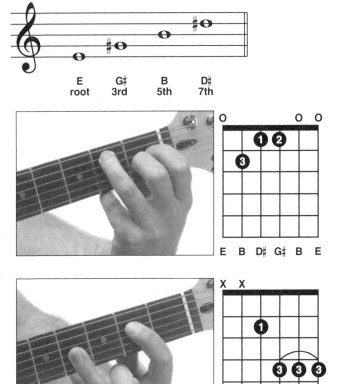

O   O O

E B D# G# B E

X X

E B D# G#

Emaj9 (EM9)

E major ninth

E	G#	B	D#	F#
root	3rd	5th	7th	9th

E B D# G# B F#

E G# D# F#

Emaj7#11 (EM7#11)

E major seventh, sharp eleventh

E	G#	B	D#	A#
root	3rd	5th	7th	#11th

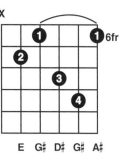

E B E A# D# G#

E G# D# G# A#

Emaj13 (EM13)

E major thirteenth

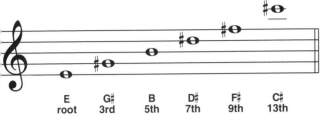

E	G#	B	D#	F#	C#
root	3rd	5th	7th	9th	13th

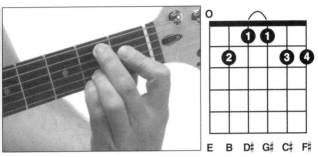

O

E B D# G# C# F#

X   X

4fr

E G# C# D#

E

Em (Emin, E-)

E minor

E	G	B
root	b3rd	5th

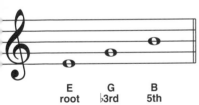

O   O O O

E B E G B E

X X

E B E G

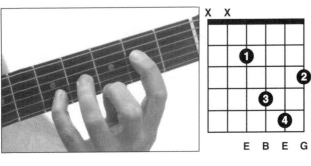

Em(add9)

E minor, added ninth

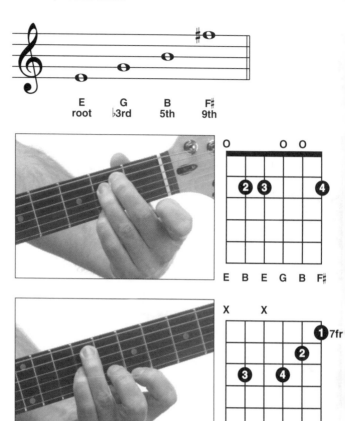

E	G	B	F#
root	♭3rd	5th	9th

E B E G B F#

F#   E G B

Em6 (Emin6, E-6)

E minor sixth

E	G	B	C#
root	♭3rd	5th	6th

E B E G C# E

E B C# G

Em♭6 (E-(♭6), Emin♭6)

minor, flat sixth

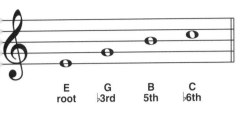

E	G	B	C
root	♭3rd	5th	♭6th

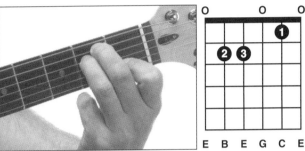

O   O   O

E B E G C E

X   5fr

E G C E B

E

Em6/9

E minor sixth, added ninth

E	G	B	C#	F#
root	♭3rd	5th	6th	9th

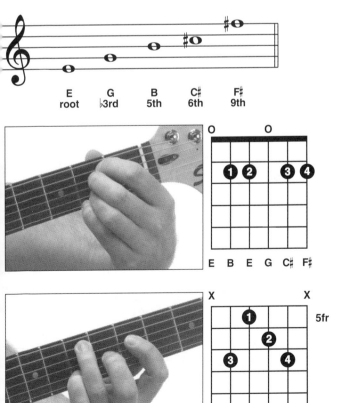

O   O

E B E G C# F#

X   X   5fr

E G C# F#

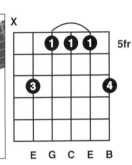

Em7 (Emin7, E-7)
E minor seventh

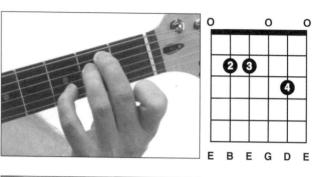

E	G	B	D
root	♭3rd	5th	♭7th

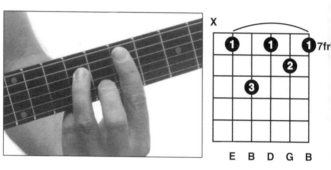

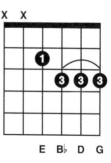

E B E G D E

E B D G B

Em7♭5 (E-7♭5, Emin7-5)
E minor seventh, flat fifth

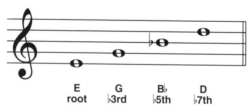

E	G	B♭	D
root	♭3rd	♭5th	♭7th

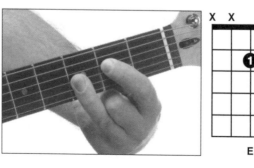

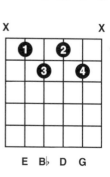

E B♭ D G

E B♭ D G

Em(maj7) (E-(+7))

E minor, major seventh

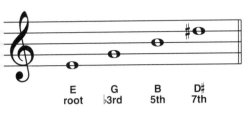

E	G	B	D#
root	♭3rd	5th	7th

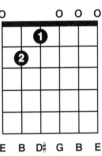

E B D# G B E

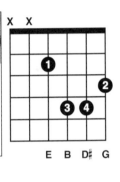

E

E B D# G

Em9 (Emin9, E-9)

E minor ninth

E	G	B	D	F#
root	♭3rd	5th	♭7th	9th

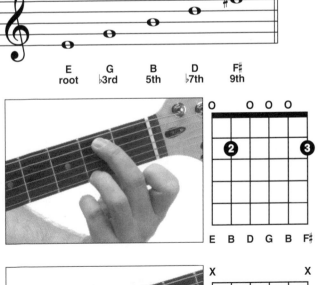

E B D G B F#

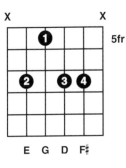

5fr

E G D F#

Em9♭5 (Em9-5, Emin9♭5)

E minor ninth, flat fifth

E	G	B♭	D	F#
root	♭3rd	♭5th	♭7th	9th

E B♭ D G D F#

G F# B♭ D

Em9(maj7) (Em9+7, E-9+7)

E minor ninth, major seventh

E	G	B	D#	F#
root	♭3rd	5th	7th	9th

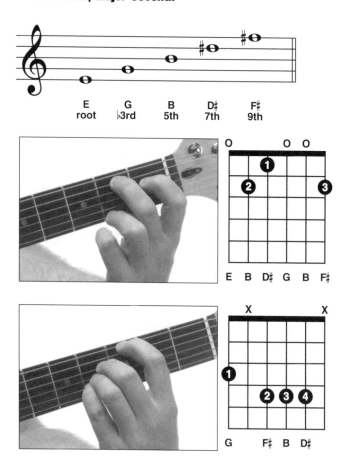

E B D# G B F#

G F# B D#

Em11 (E-11, Emin11)

E minor eleventh

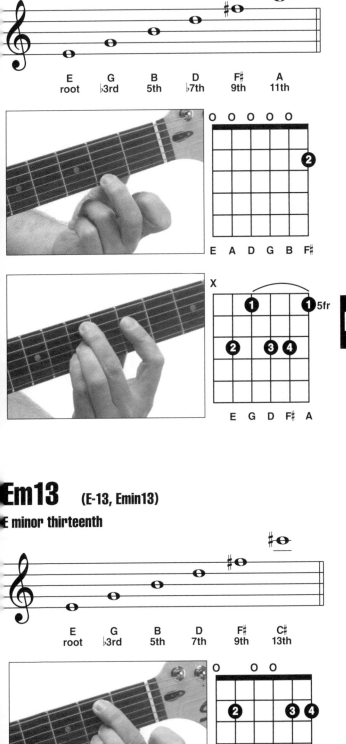

E	G	B	D	F♯	A
root	♭3rd	5th	♭7th	9th	11th

E A D G B F♯

E G D F♯ A

Em13 (E-13, Emin13)

E minor thirteenth

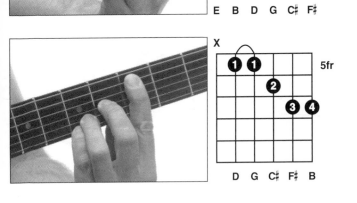

E	G	B	D	F♯	C♯
root	♭3rd	5th	7th	9th	13th

E B D G C♯ F♯

D G C♯ F♯ B

E7 (Edom7)
E dominant seventh

E	G#	B	D
root	3rd	5th	♭7th

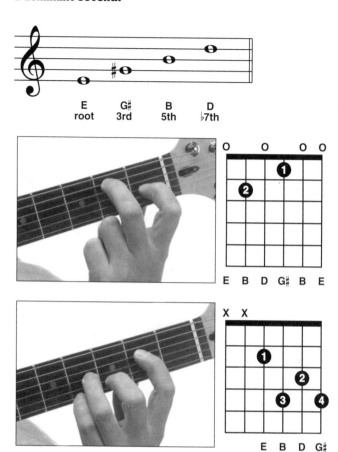

E B D G# B E

E B D G#

E7sus4 (E7sus)
E dominant seventh, suspended fourth

E	A	B	D
root	4th	5th	♭7th

E B D A B E

E B D A

E7♭5 (E7-5, Edom7♭5)
E dominant seventh, flat fifth

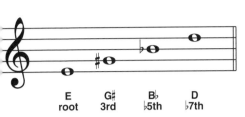

E	G#	B♭	D
root	3rd	♭5th	♭7th

X X

E B♭ D G#

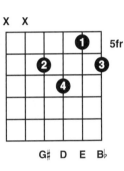

X X · 5fr

G# D E B♭

E

E9
E ninth

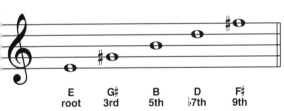

E	G#	B	D	F#
root	3rd	5th	♭7th	9th

O O O

E B D G# B F#

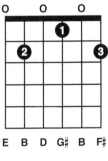

X X · 9fr

E D F# G#

E9sus4 (E9sus)

E ninth, suspended fourth

E	A	B	D	F#
root	4th	5th	♭7th	9th

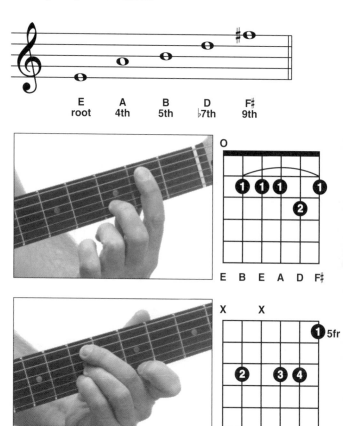

E B E A D F#

E D F# A

E7♭9 (E7-9, Edom7♭9)

E dominant seventh, flat ninth

E	G#	B	D	F
root	3rd	5th	♭7th	♭9th

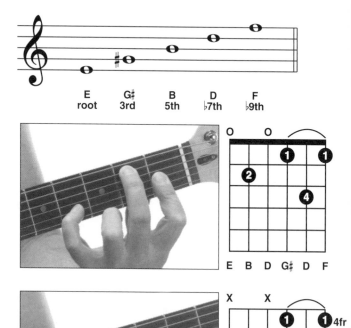

E B D G# D F

D B F G#

E7♯9 (E7+9, Edom7♯9)
E dominant seventh, sharp ninth

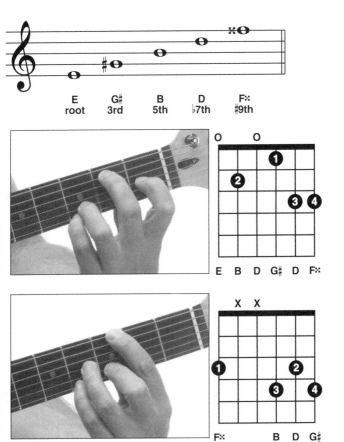

E	G♯	B	D	F𝄪
root	3rd	5th	♭7th	♯9th

E B D G♯ D F𝄪

F𝄪 B D G♯

E7♭5(♯9) (E7-5(+9), Edom7♭5(♯9))
E dominant seventh, flat fifth, sharp ninth

E	G♯	B♭	D	F𝄪
root	3rd	♭5th	♭7th	♯9th

E B♭ E G♯ D F𝄪

F𝄪 B♭ D G♯

E

E11
E eleventh

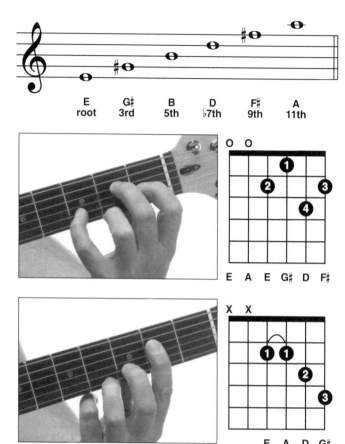

E	G#	B	D	F#	A
root	3rd	5th	♭7th	9th	11th

E7#11 (E7+11, Edom7#11)
E dominant seventh, sharp eleventh

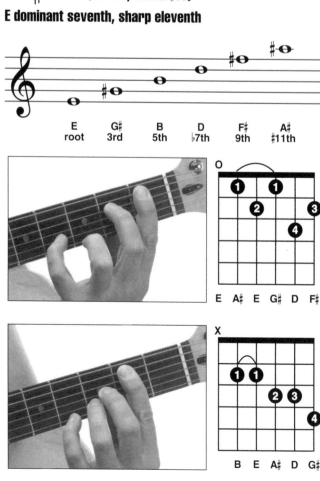

E	G#	B	D	F#	A#
root	3rd	5th	♭7th	9th	#11th

E13 (Edom13)

E thirteenth

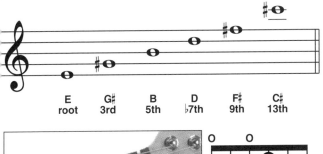

E	G#	B	D	F#	C#
root	3rd	5th	♭7th	9th	13th

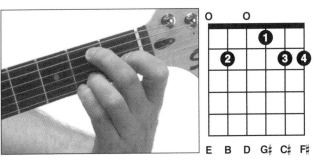

E B D G# C# F#

X   X   5fr

D G# C# E

E

E13sus4 (E13sus)

E thirteenth, suspended fourth

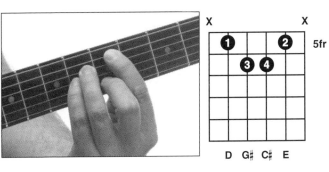

E	A	B	D	F#	C#
root	4th	5th	♭7th	9th	13th

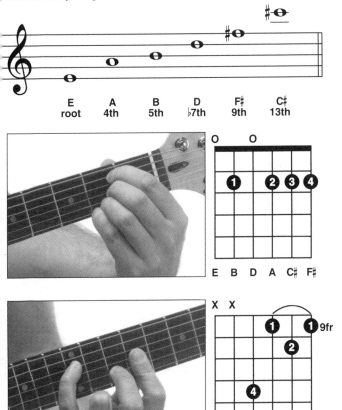

E B D A C# F#

X X   9fr

D E A C#

E+ (Eaug, E(♯5))
E augmented

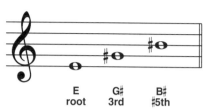

E root / G♯ 3rd / B♯ ♯5th

X X   O

E G♯ B♯ E

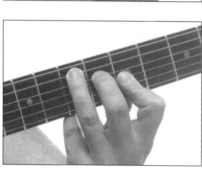

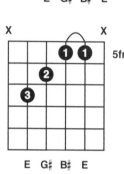

X   X   5fr

E G♯ B♯ E

E+7 (E7♯5)
E seventh, sharp fifth

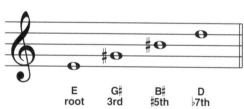

E root / G♯ 3rd / B♯ ♯5th / D ♭7th

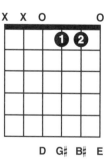

X X O   O

D G♯ B♯ E

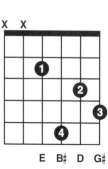

X X

E B♯ D G♯

E° (Edim)

E diminished

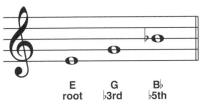

E	G	B♭
root	♭3rd	♭5th

X X

E B♭ E G

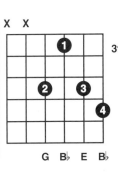

X X 3fr

E

G B♭ E B♭

E°7 (Edim7)

E diminished seventh

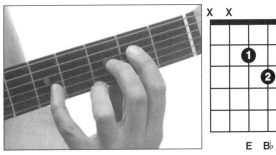

E	G	B♭	D♭
root	♭3rd	♭5th	♭♭7th

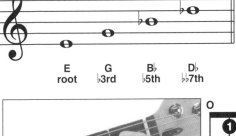

O   O   O

E B♭ E G D♭ E

X X

E B♭ D♭ G

F (Fmaj)

F major

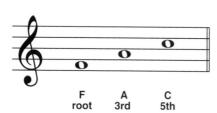

F	A	C
root	3rd	5th

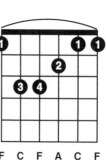

F C F A C F

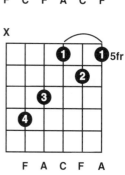

X ... 5fr

F A C F A

F5 (F(no3rd))

F fifth (power chord)

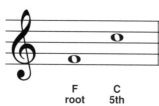

F	C
root	5th

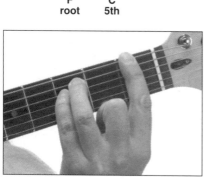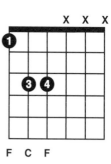

X X X

F C F

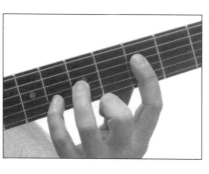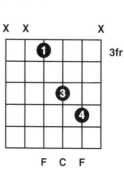

X X ... X 3fr

F C F

Fsus4 (Fsus)

F suspended fourth

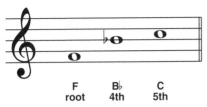

F	B♭	C
root	4th	5th

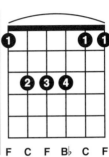

F C F B♭ C F

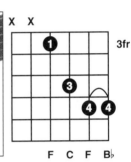

X X

3fr

F C F B♭

F

Fsus2 (F5add2)

F suspended second

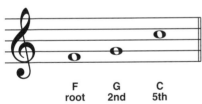

F	G	C
root	2nd	5th

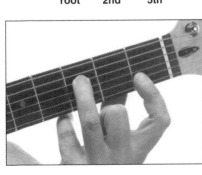

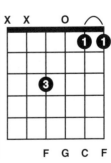

X X O

F G C F

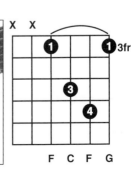

X X

3fr

F C F G

Fadd9

F added ninth

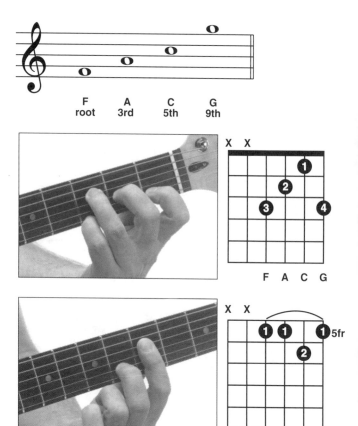

F	A	C	G
root	3rd	5th	9th

X X

F A C G

X X

5fr

G C F A

F6

F sixth

F	A	C	D
root	3rd	5th	6th

X O X

F D A C

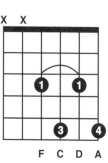

X X

F C D A

F6/9 (F6add9)
F sixth, added ninth

F	A	C	D	G
root	3rd	5th	6th	9th

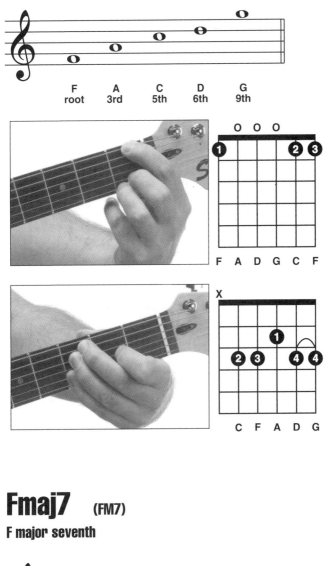

F A D G C F

C F A D G

Fmaj7 (FM7)
F major seventh

F	A	C	E
root	3rd	5th	7th

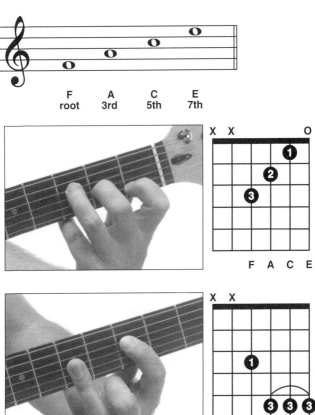

F A C E

F C E A

Fmaj9 (FM9)

F major ninth

F	A	C	E	G
root	3rd	5th	7th	9th

F A E G C E

F A E G

Fmaj7♯11 (FM7♯11)

F major seventh, sharp eleventh

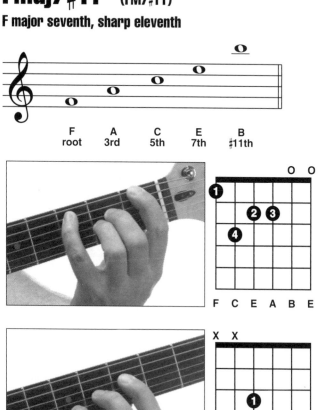

F	A	C	E	B
root	3rd	5th	7th	♯11th

F C E A B E

F B E A

Fmaj13 (FM13)
F major thirteenth

F	A	C	E	G	D
root	3rd	5th	7th	9th	13th

O O O O

F A D G C E

X

5fr

F A D E A

F

Fm (Fmin, F-)
F minor

F	A♭	C
root	♭3rd	5th

F C F A♭ C F

X X

3fr

F C F A♭

Fm(add 9)

F minor, added ninth

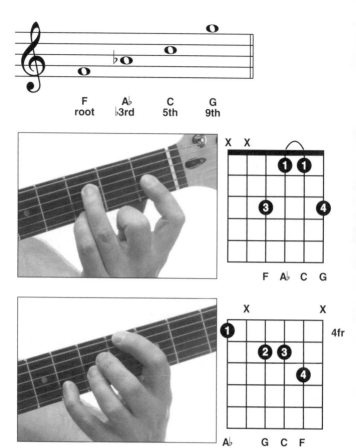

F	A♭	C	G
root	♭3rd	5th	9th

Fm6 (Fmin6, F-6)

F minor sixth

F	A♭	C	D
root	♭3rd	5th	6th

Fm♭6 (F-(♭6), Fmin♭6)
F minor, flat sixth

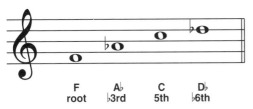

F	A♭	C	D♭
root	♭3rd	5th	♭6th

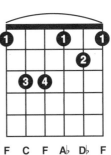

F C F A♭ D♭ F

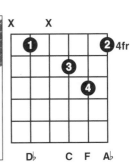

D♭ C F A♭

F

Fm6/9
F minor sixth, added ninth

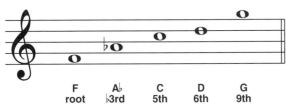

F	A♭	C	D	G
root	♭3rd	5th	6th	9th

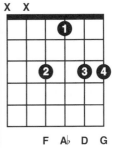

F A♭ D G

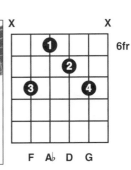

F A♭ D G

Fm7 (F-7, Fmin7)
F minor seventh

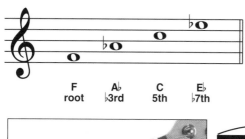

F	A♭	C	E♭
root	♭3rd	5th	♭7th

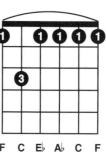

F C E♭ A♭ C F

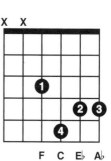

F C E♭ A♭

Fm7♭5 (F-7♭5, Fmin7-5)
F minor seventh, flat fifth

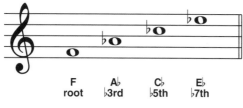

F	A♭	C♭	E♭
root	♭3rd	♭5th	♭7th

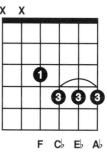

F C♭ E♭ A♭

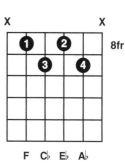

8fr

F C♭ E♭ A♭

Fm(maj7) (Fm(+7))

F minor, major seventh

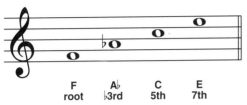

F	A♭	C	E
root	♭3rd	5th	7th

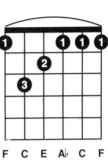

F C E A♭ C F

X X

F C E A♭

F

Fm9 (F-9, Fmin9)

F minor ninth

F	A♭	C	E♭	G
root	♭3rd	5th	♭7th	9th

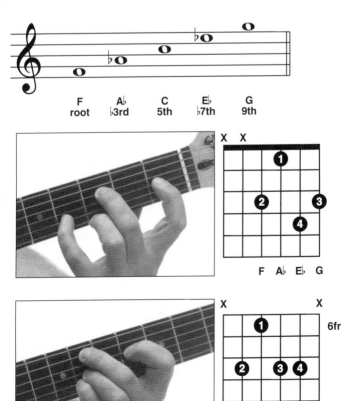

X X

F A♭ E♭ G

X   X

6fr

F A♭ E♭ G

Fm9♭5 (Fm9-5, Fmin9♭5)

F minor ninth, flat fifth

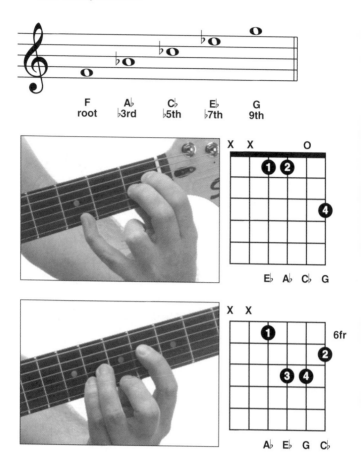

F	A♭	C♭	E♭	G
root	♭3rd	♭5th	♭7th	9th

X X   O

E♭ A♭ C♭ G

X X

6fr

A♭ E♭ G C♭

Fm9(maj7) (Fm9+7, F-9+7)

F minor ninth, major seventh

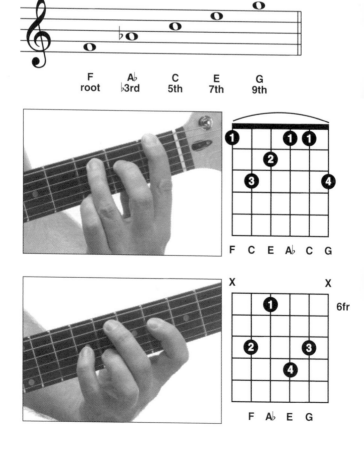

F	A♭	C	E	G
root	♭3rd	5th	7th	9th

F C E A♭ C G

X   X

6fr

F A♭ E G

Fm11   (F-11, Fmin11)
F minor eleventh

F	A♭	C	E♭	G	B♭
root	♭3rd	5th	♭7th	9th	11th

F B♭ E♭ A♭ C G

F B♭ E♭ A♭

Fm13   (F-13, Fmin13)
F minor thirteenth

F	A♭	C	E♭	G	D
root	♭3rd	5th	♭7th	9th	13th

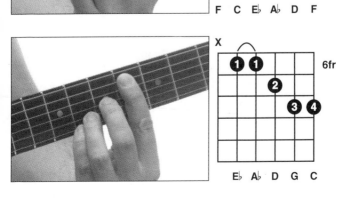

F C E♭ A♭ D F

E♭ A♭ D G C

6fr

F

F7 (Fdom7)
F dominant seventh

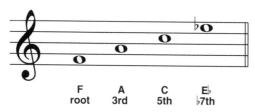

F	A	C	E♭
root	3rd	5th	♭7th

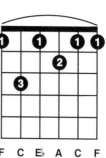

F C E♭ A C F

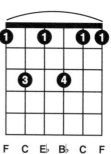

X X

F C E♭ A

F7sus4 (F7sus)
F dominant seventh, suspended fourth

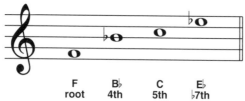

F	B♭	C	E♭
root	4th	5th	♭7th

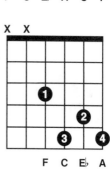

F C E♭ B♭ C F

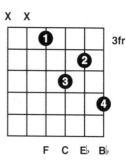

X X

3fr

F C E♭ B♭

F7♭5 (F7-5, Fdom7♭5)

F dominant seventh, flat fifth

F	A	C♭	E♭
root	3rd	♭5th	♭7th

E♭ A C♭ F

F C♭ E♭ A

F9

F ninth

F	A	C	E♭	G
root	3rd	5th	♭7th	9th

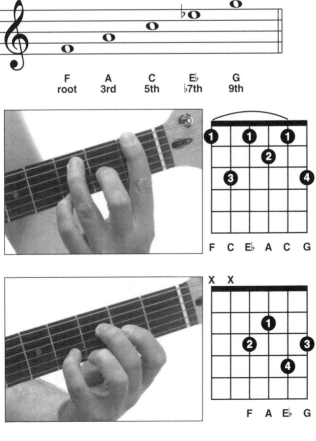

F C E♭ A C G

F A E♭ G

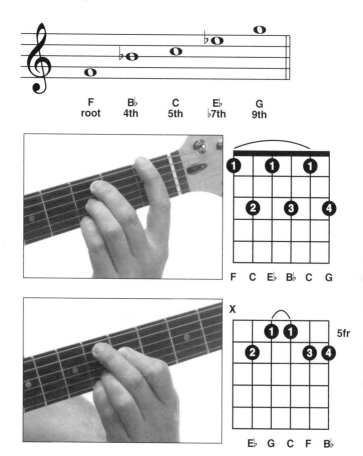

F9sus4 (F9sus)
F ninth, suspended fourth

F	B♭	C	E♭	G
root	4th	5th	♭7th	9th

F C E♭ B♭ C G

X
5fr

E♭ G C F B♭

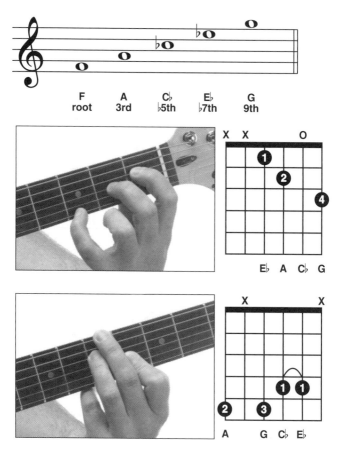

F9♭5 (F9-5, Fdom9♭5)
F ninth, flat fifth

F	A	C♭	E♭	G
root	3rd	♭5th	♭7th	9th

X X O

E♭ A C♭ G

X X

A G C♭ E♭

F7♭9 (F7-9, Fdom7♭9)
F dominant seventh, flat ninth

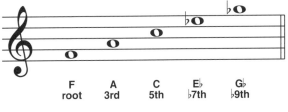

F	A	C	E♭	G♭
root	3rd	5th	♭7th	♭9th

F7♯9 (F7+9, Fdom7♯9)
F dominant seventh, sharp ninth

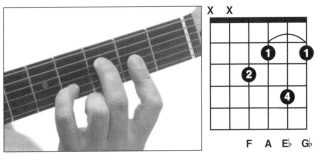

F	A	C	E♭	G♯
root	3rd	5th	♭7th	♯9th

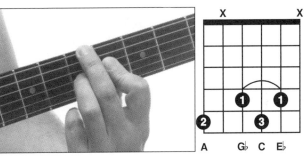

F

F7♭5(♯9) (F7-5 (+9), Fdom7♭5(♯9))

F dominant seventh, flat fifth, sharp ninth

F	A	C♭	E♭	G♯
root	3rd	♭5th	♭7th	♯9th

E♭ A C♭ G♯

F A E♭ G♯ C♭

F11

F eleventh

F	A	C	E♭	G	B♭
root	3rd	5th	♭7th	9th	11th

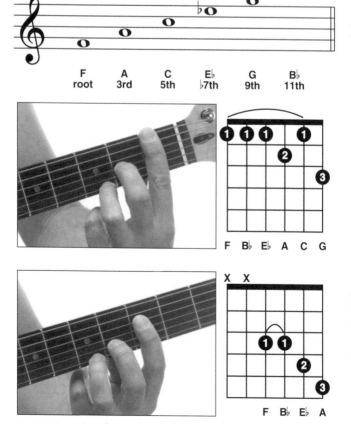

F B♭ E♭ A C G

F B♭ E♭ A

F7#11 (F7+11, Fdom7#11)

F dominant seventh, sharp eleventh

F	A	C	E♭	B
root	3rd	5th	♭7th	#11th

F B E♭ A C F

C F B E♭ A

F13 (Fdom13)

F thirteenth

F	A	C	E♭	G	D
root	3rd	5th	♭7th	9th	13th

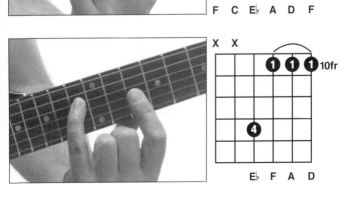

F C E♭ A D F

E♭ F A D

F

F13sus4 (F13sus)
F thirteenth, suspended fourth

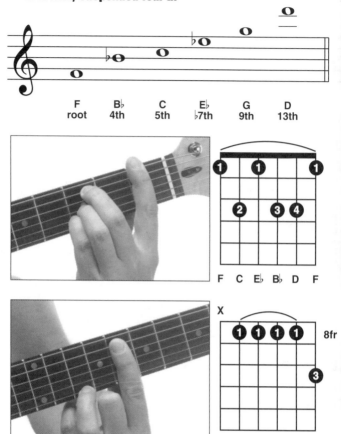

F	B♭	C	E♭	G	D
root	4th	5th	♭7th	9th	13th

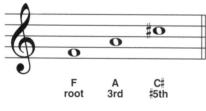

F C E♭ B♭ D F

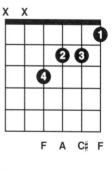

8fr

F B♭ E♭ G D

F+ (Faug, F(♯5))
F augmented

F	A	C♯
root	3rd	♯5th

F A C♯ F

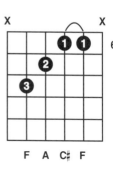

6fr

F A C♯ F

F+7 (F7#5)

F dominant seventh, sharp fifth

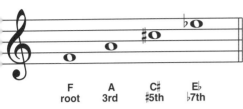

F	A	C#	Eb
root	3rd	#5th	b7th

Eb A C# F

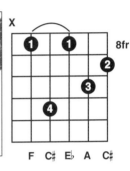

F C# Eb A C#

8fr

F° (Fdim)

F diminished

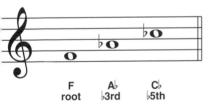

F	Ab	Cb
root	b3rd	b5th

F Ab Cb F

Ab Cb F Ab

4fr

F

F°7 (Fdim7)

F diminished seventh

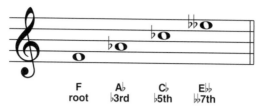

F	A♭	C♭	E♭♭
root	♭3rd	♭5th	♭♭7th

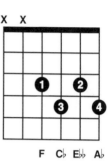

F C♭ E♭♭ A♭

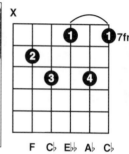

F C♭ E♭♭ A♭ C♭

F# (F#maj)
F-sharp major

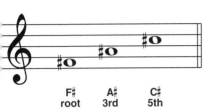

F#   A#   C#
root   3rd   5th

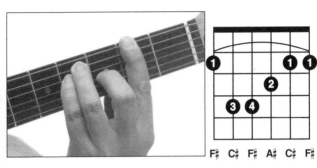

F# C# F# A# C# F#

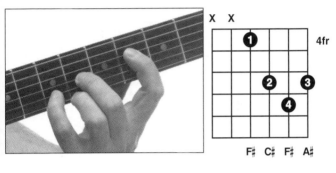

F# C# F# A#

F#5 (F#(no3rd))
F-sharp fifth (power chord)

F#   C#
root   5th

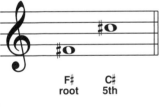

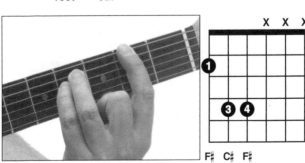

F# C# F#

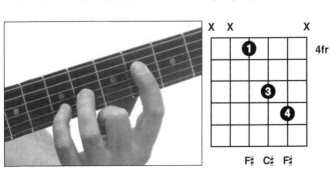

F# C# F#

F#sus4 (F#sus)
F-sharp suspended fourth

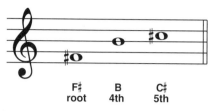

	F#	B	C#
	root	4th	5th

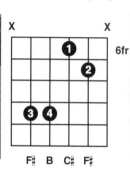

F# C# F# B C# F#

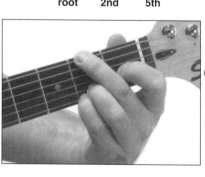

X   X
6fr

F# B C# F#

F#sus2 (F#5add2)
F-sharp suspended second

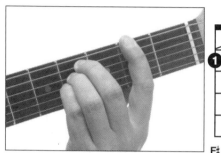

	F#	G#	C#
	root	2nd	5th

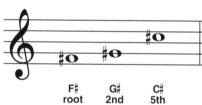

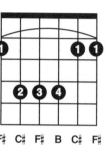

X X

F#   G# C# F#

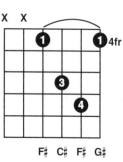

X X
4fr

F# C# F# G#

F#add9

F-sharp added ninth

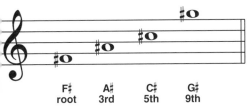

F#	A#	C#	G#
root	3rd	5th	9th

X X

F# A# C# G#

X X

6fr

G# C# F# A#

F#6

F-sharp sixth

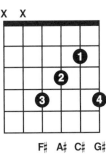

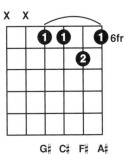

F#	A#	C#	D#
root	3rd	5th	6th

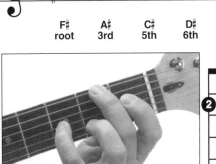

X X

F# D# A#

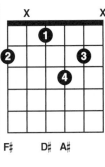

X

9fr

F# C# F# A# D#

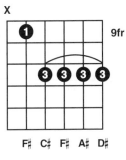

F#6/9 (F#6 add 9)
F-sharp sixth, added ninth

F#	A#	C#	D#	G#
root	3rd	5th	6th	9th

F# A# D# G# C# F#

C# F# A# D# G#

F#maj7 (F#M7)
F-sharp major seventh

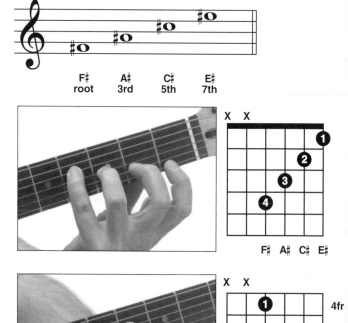

F#	A#	C#	E#
root	3rd	5th	7th

F# A# C# E#

F# C# E# A#

♯maj9 (F♯M9)
F-sharp major ninth

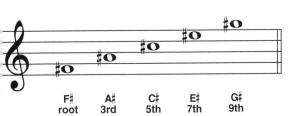

F♯	A♯	C♯	E♯	G♯
root	3rd	5th	7th	9th

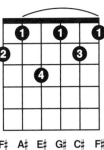

F♯ A♯ E♯ G♯ C♯ F♯

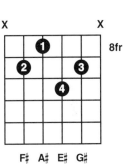

8fr

F♯ A♯ E♯ G♯

F♯maj7♯11 (F♯M7♯11)
F-sharp major seventh, sharp eleventh

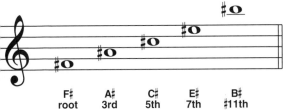

F♯	A♯	C♯	E♯	B♯
root	3rd	5th	7th	♯11th

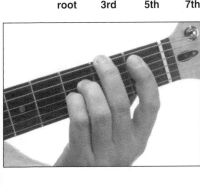

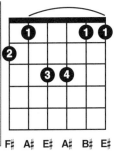

F♯ A♯ E♯ A♯ B♯ E♯

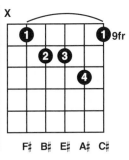

9fr

F♯ B♯ E♯ A♯ C♯

F#maj13 (F#M13)
F-sharp major thirteenth

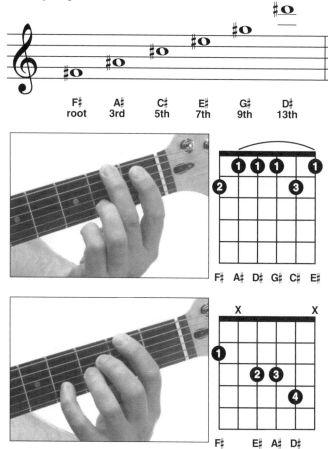

F#	A#	C#	E#	G#	D#
root	3rd	5th	7th	9th	13th

F# A# D# G# C# E#

X   X

F#   E# A# D#

F#m (F#-, F#min)
F-sharp minor

F#	A	C#
root	♭3rd	5th

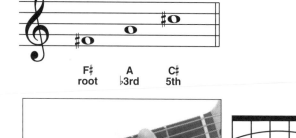

F# C# F# A C# F#

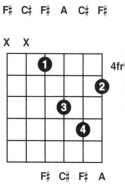
X   X

4fr

F# C# F# A

F#m(add9)

F-sharp minor, added ninth

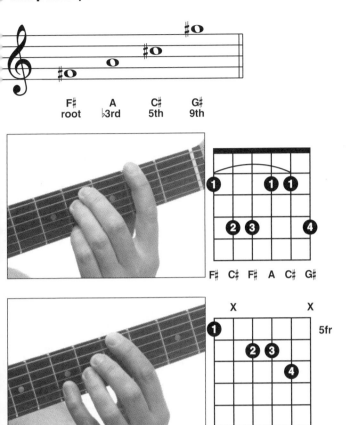

F#	A	C#	G#
root	b3rd	5th	9th

F# C# F# A C# G#

X X

5fr

A ..... G# C# F#

F#m6 (F#-6, F#min6)

F-sharp minor sixth

F#	A	C#	D#
root	b3rd	5th	6th

F# C# F# A D# F#

X X

4fr

F# C# D# A

F#m♭6 (F#-(♭6), F#min♭6)
F-sharp minor, flat sixth

F#	A	C#	D
root	♭3rd	5th	♭6th

F# C# F# A D F#

X

9fr

F# C# F# A D

F#m6/9
F-sharp minor sixth, added ninth

F#	A	C#	D#	G#
root	♭3rd	5th	6th	9th

X X

F# A D# G#

X X

5fr

G# D# F# A

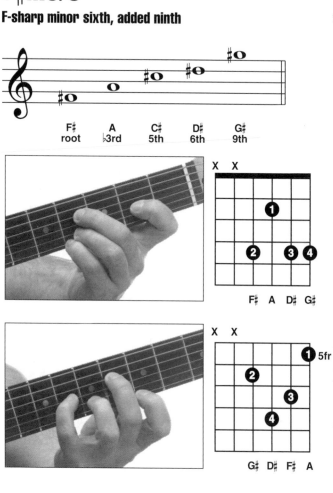

F#m7 (F#–7, F#min7)
F-sharp minor seventh

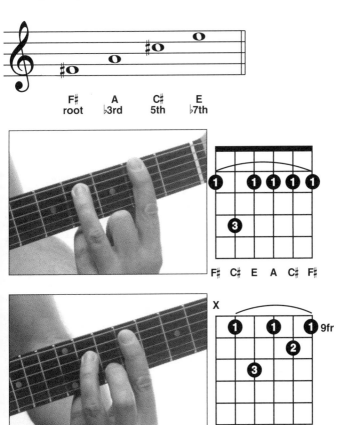

F#	A	C#	E
root	b3rd	5th	b7th

F# C# E A C# F#

X ... 9fr

F# C# E A C#

F#m7b5 (F#–7b5, F#min7-5)
F-sharp minor seventh, flat fifth

F#	A	C	E
root	b3rd	b5th	b7th

X ... X

F# E A C

X ... X ... 9fr

F# C E A

F#m(maj7) (F#m(+7))
F-sharp minor, major seventh

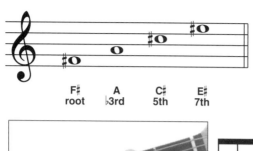

F#	A	C#	E#
root	b3rd	5th	7th

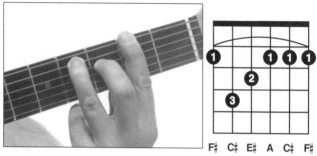

F# C# E# A C# F#

X 9fr

F# C# E# A C#

F#m9 (F#–9, F#min9)
F-sharp minor ninth

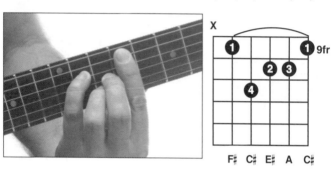

F#	A	C#	E	G#
root	b3rd	5th	b7th	9th

F# C# E A C# G#

X X

F# A E G#

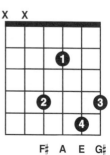

F#m9♭5 (F#m9-5, F#min9♭5)
F-sharp minor ninth, flat fifth

F#	A	C	E	G#
root	♭3rd	♭5th	♭7th	9th

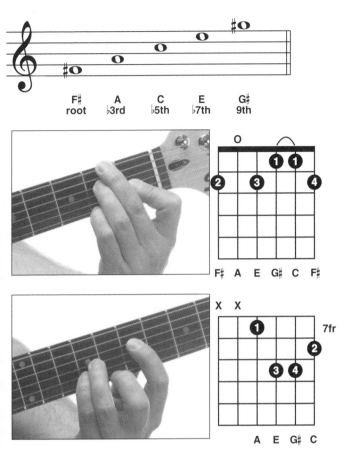

F# A E G# C F#

A E G# C

F#m9(maj7) (F#m9+7, F#-9+7)
F-sharp minor ninth, major seventh

F#	A	C#	E#	G#
root	♭3rd	5th	7th	9th

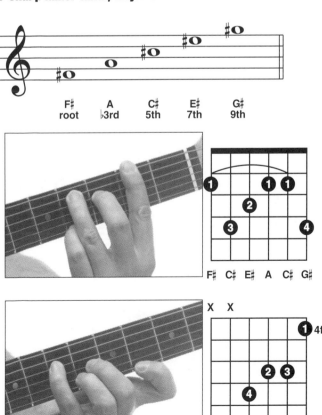

F# C# E# A C# G#

A C# E# G#

F#m11 (F#-11, F#min11)
F-sharp minor eleventh

F#	A	C#	E	G#	B
root	♭3rd	5th	♭7th	9th	11th

F# B E A C# G#

7fr

F# A E G# B

F#m13 (F#-13, F#min13)
F-sharp minor thirteenth

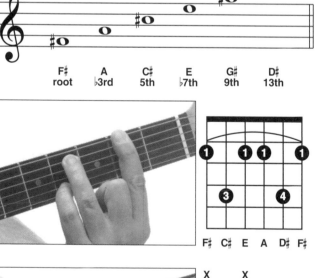

F#	A	C#	E	G#	D#
root	♭3rd	5th	♭7th	9th	13th

F# C# E A D# F#

9fr

F# E A D#

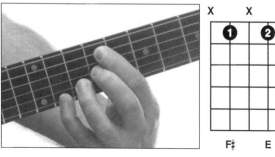

F#7 (F#dom7)
F-sharp dominant seventh

F#	A#	C#	E
root	3rd	5th	b7th

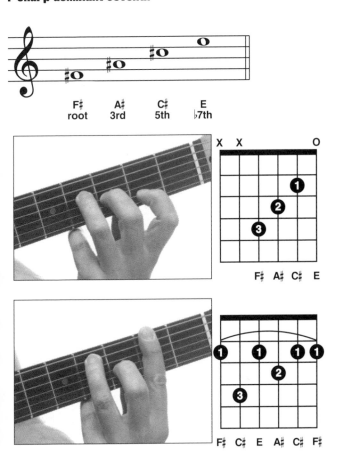

F#7sus4 (F#7sus)
F-sharp dominant seventh, suspended fourth

F#	B	C#	E
root	4th	5th	b7th

F#

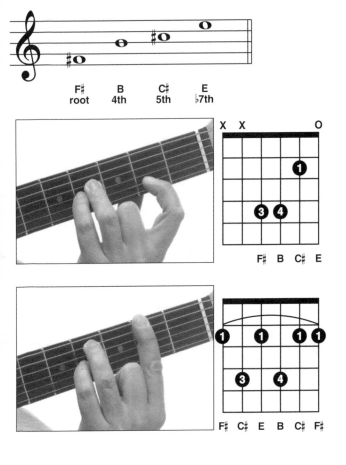

F#7♭5 (F#7-5, F#dom7♭5)
F-sharp dominant seventh, flat fifth

F#	A#	C	E
root	3rd	♭5th	♭7th

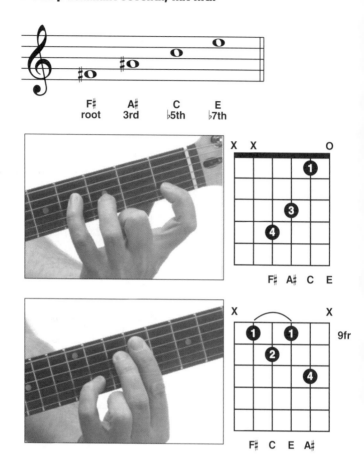

F# A# C E

F# C E A# 9fr

F#9
F-sharp ninth

F#	A#	C#	E	G#
root	3rd	5th	♭7th	9th

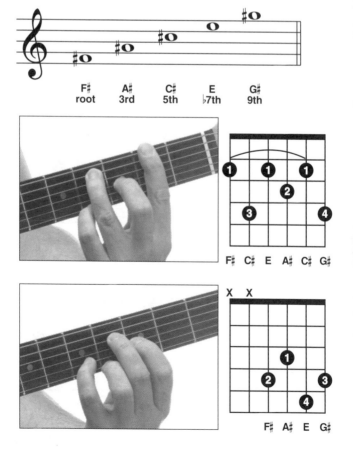

F# C# E A# C# G#

F# A# E G#

F#9sus4 (F#9sus)

F-sharp ninth, suspended fourth

F#	B	C#	E	G#
root	4th	5th	♭7th	9th

F# C# E B C# G#

X X

F# B E G#

F#7♭9 (F#7−9, F#dom7♭9)

F-sharp dominant seventh, flat ninth

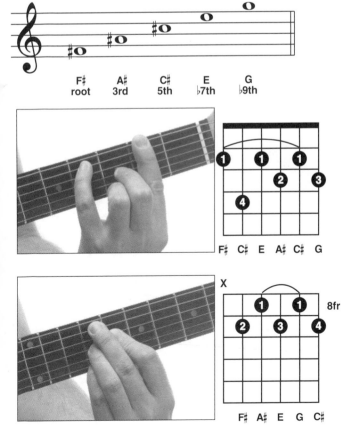

F#	A#	C#	E	G
root	3rd	5th	♭7th	♭9th

F# C# E A# C# G

X

8fr

F# A# E G C#

F#7#9 (F#7+9, F#dom7#9)
F-sharp dominant seventh, sharp ninth

F#	A#	C#	E	G×
root	3rd	5th	♭7th	#9th

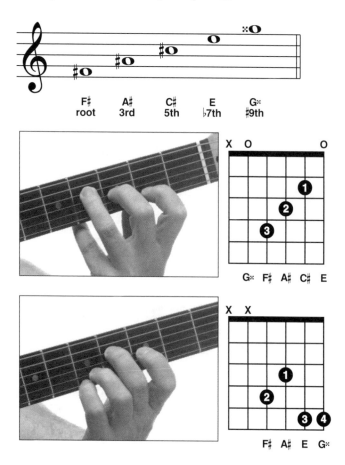

G× F# A# C# E

F# A# E G×

F#7♭5(#9) (F#7−5(+9), F#dom7♭5(#9))
F-sharp dominant seventh, flat fifth, sharp ninth

F#	A#	C	E	G×
root	3rd	♭5th	♭7th	#9th

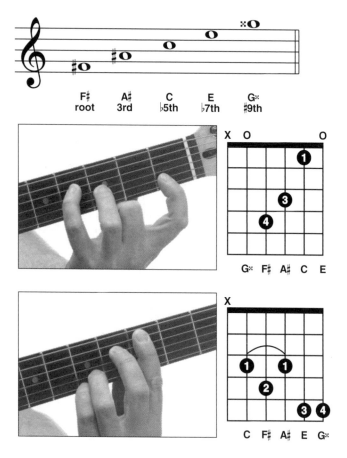

G× F# A# C E

C F# A# E G×

F#11

F-sharp eleventh

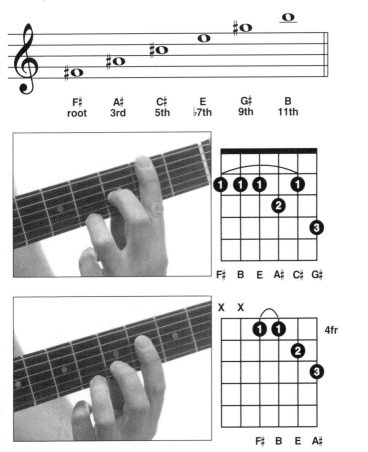

F#	A#	C#	E	G#	B
root	3rd	5th	♭7th	9th	11th

F# B E A# C# G#

X X   4fr

F# B E A#

F#7#11   (F#7+11, F#dom7#11)

F-sharp dominant seventh, sharp eleventh

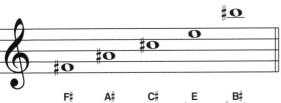

F#	A#	C#	E	B#
root	3rd	5th	♭7th	#11th

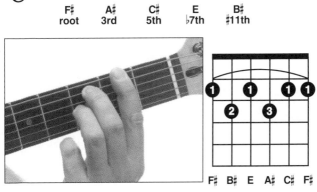

F# B# E A# C# F#

X   9fr

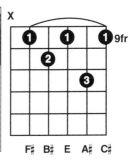

F# B# E A# C#

F#13 (F#dom13)
F-sharp thirteenth

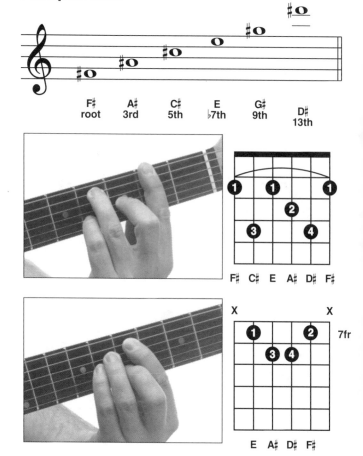

F# root	A# 3rd	C# 5th	E ♭7th	G# 9th	D# 13th

F# C# E A# D# F#

X   X   7fr

E A# D# F#

F#13sus4 (F#13sus)
F-sharp thirteenth, suspended fourth

F# root	B 4th	C# 5th	E ♭7th	G# 9th	D# 13th

F# C# E B D# F#

X   X   11fr

E   F# B D#

F#+ (F#aug, F#(#5))
F-sharp augmented

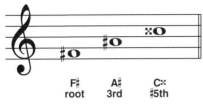

F#   A#   Cx
root   3rd   #5th

X X O

Cx A# Cx F#

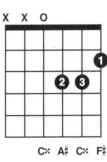

X X

5fr

Cx   Cx F# A#

F#+7 (F#7#5)
F-sharp dominant seventh, sharp fifth

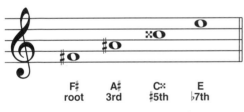

F#   A#   Cx   E
root   3rd   #5th   b7th

X X   O

F# A# Cx E

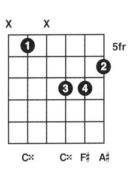

X   X

7fr

E A# Cx F#

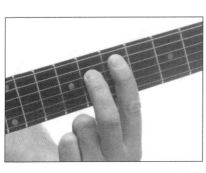

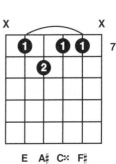

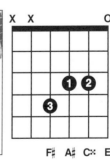

F#° (F#dim)
F-sharp diminished

F#	A	C
root	♭3rd	♭5th

X X

F#   A   C F#

X X

5fr

A C F# A

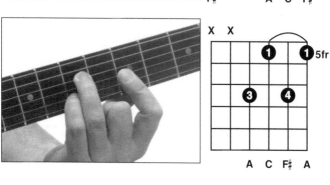

F#°7 (F#dim7)
F-sharp diminished seventh

F#	A	C	E♭
root	♭3rd	♭5th	♭♭7th

O

F# A E♭ A C F#

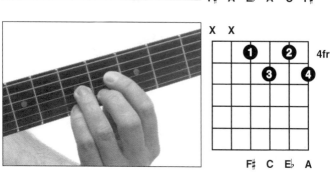

X X

4fr

F# C E♭ A

G (Gmaj)
G major

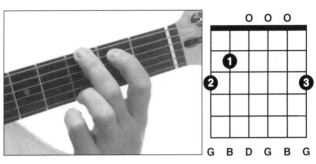

G	B	D
root	3rd	5th

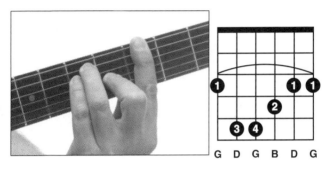

O O O

G B D G B G

G D G B D G

G5 (G5(no 3rd))
G fifth (power chord)

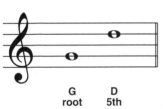

G	D
root	5th

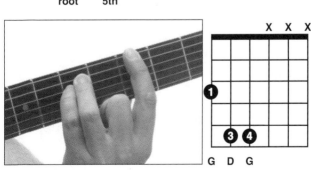

X X X

G D G

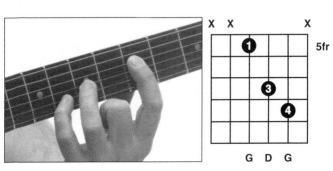

X X X

5fr

G D G

G

Gsus4 (Gsus)

G suspended fourth

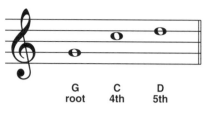

G C D
root 4th 5th

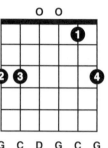

O O

G C D G C G

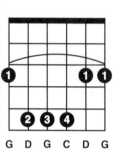

G D G C D G

Gsus2 (G5add2)

G suspended second

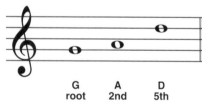

G A D
root 2nd 5th

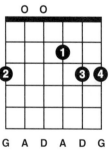

O O

G A D A D G

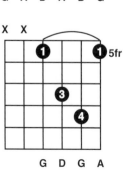

X X

5fr

G D G A

Gadd9
G added ninth

G	B	D	A
root	3rd	5th	9th

O O   O

G A D A B G

X X

G B D A

G6
G sixth

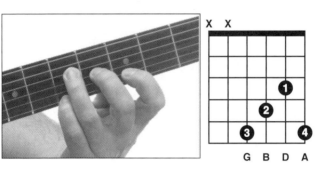

G	B	D	E
root	3rd	5th	6th

G

O O O O

G B D G B E

X X

5fr

G D E B

G6/9 (G6add9)
G sixth, added ninth

G root	B 3rd	D 5th	E 6th	A 9th

G B D A B E

E A D G B 7fr

Gmaj7 (GM7)
G major seventh

G root	B 3rd	D 5th	F♯ 7th

G B D G B F♯

G F♯ B D

Gmaj9 (GM9)

G major ninth

G	B	D	F#	A
root	3rd	5th	7th	9th

G A D A B F#

9fr

G B F# A

Gmaj7#11 (GM7#11)

G major seventh, sharp eleventh

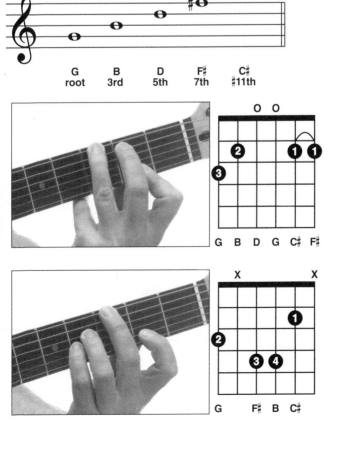

G	B	D	F#	C#
root	3rd	5th	7th	#11th

G

G B D G C# F#

X X

G F# B C#

Gmaj13 (GM13)
G major thirteenth

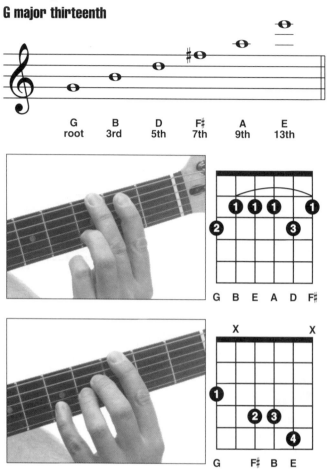

G	B	D	F#	A	E
root	3rd	5th	7th	9th	13th

G B E A D F#

X   X

G   F# B E

Gm (G-, Gmin)
G minor

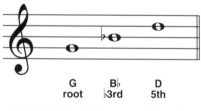

G	Bb	D
root	b3rd	5th

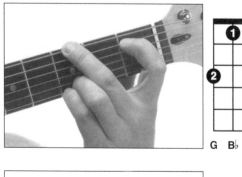

O O

G Bb D G D G

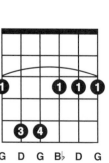

G D G Bb D G

Gm(add9)

G minor, added ninth

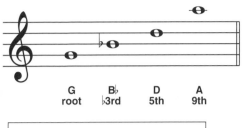

G	B♭	D	A
root	♭3rd	5th	9th

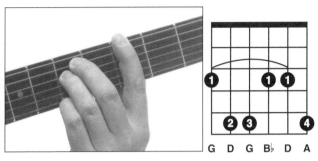

G D G B♭ D A

X X

B♭ D G A

5fr

Gm6 (G-6, Gmin6)

G minor sixth

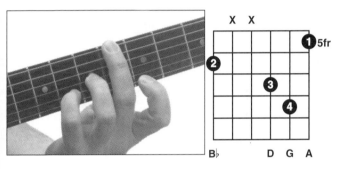

G	B♭	D	E
root	♭3rd	5th	6th

G

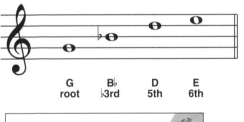

O O

G B♭ D B♭ D E

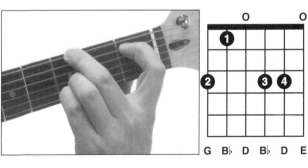

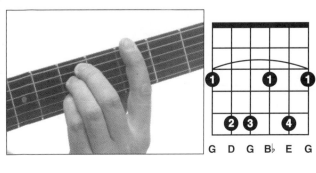

G D G B♭ E G

Gm♭6 (G-(♭6), Gmin♭6)

G minor, flat sixth

G	B♭	D	E♭
root	♭3rd	5th	♭6th

G D G B♭ E♭ G

8fr

G B♭ E♭ G D

Gm6/9

G minor sixth, added ninth

G	B♭	D	E	A
root	♭3rd	5th	6th	9th

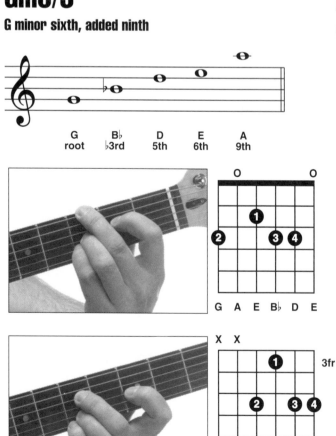

G A E B♭ D E

3fr

G B♭ E A

Gm7 (G-7, Gmin7)

G minor seventh

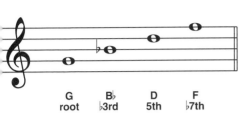

G	B♭	D	F
root	♭3rd	5th	♭7th

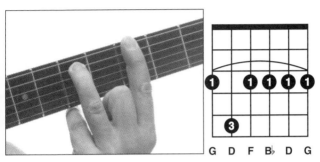

G D F B♭ D G

X X

G D F B♭

5fr

Gm7♭5 (G-7♭5, Gmin7-5)

G minor seventh, flat fifth

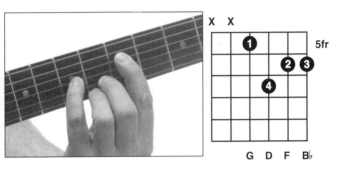

G	B♭	D♭	F
root	♭3rd	♭5th	♭7th

X   X

G F B♭ D♭

X X

5fr

G D♭ F B♭

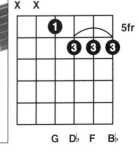

Gm(maj7) (Gm(+7))

G minor, major seventh

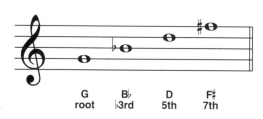

G	B♭	D	F#
root	♭3rd	5th	7th

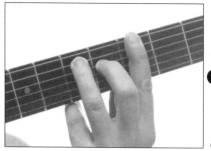

G D F# B♭ D G

X X

5fr

G D F# B♭

Gm9 (G-9, Gmin9)

G minor ninth

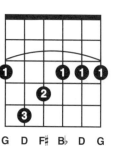

G	B♭	D	F	A
root	♭3rd	5th	♭7th	9th

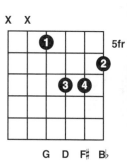

G D F B♭ D A

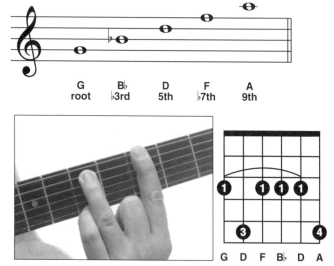

X X

8fr

G B♭ F A

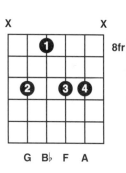

Gm9♭5 (Gm9-5, Gmin9♭5)

G minor ninth, flat fifth

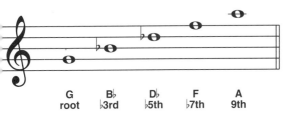

G	B♭	D♭	F	A
root	♭3rd	♭5th	♭7th	9th

X

B♭ F A D♭ F

X X

F B♭ D♭ A

Gm9(maj7) (Gm9+7, G-9+7)

G minor ninth, major seventh

G	B♭	D	F♯	A
root	♭3rd	5th	7th	9th

G

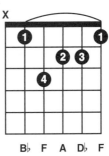

O O

G A D B♭ D F♯

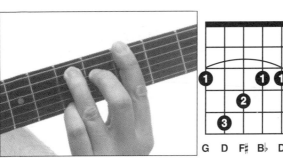

G D F♯ B♭ D A

Gm11 (G-11, Gmin11)

G minor eleventh

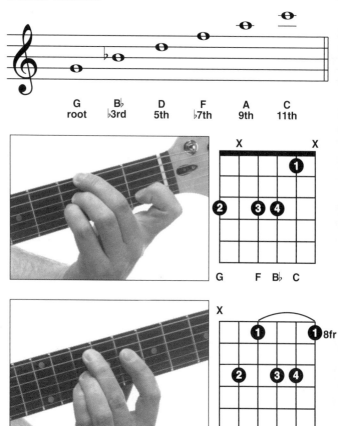

G	B♭	D	F	A	C
root	♭3rd	5th	♭7th	9th	11th

Gm13 (G-13, Gmin13)

G minor thirteenth

G	B♭	D	F	A	E
root	♭3rd	5th	♭7th	9th	13th

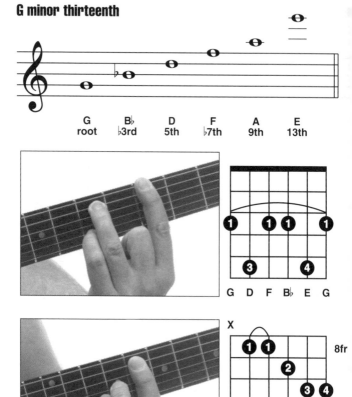

G7 (Gdom7)

G dominant seventh

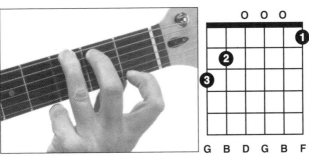

G	B	D	F
root	3rd	5th	♭7th

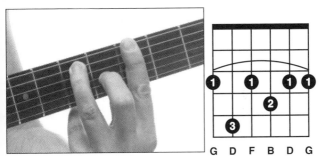

G B D G B F

G D F B D G

G7sus4 (G7sus)

G dominant seventh, suspended fourth

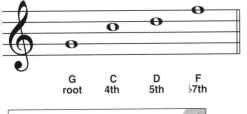

G	C	D	F
root	4th	5th	♭7th

G

G C D G C F

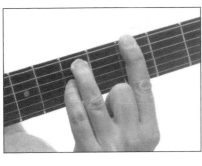

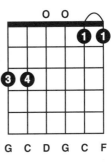

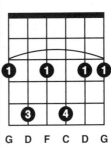

G D F C D G

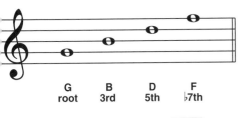

G7♭5 (G7-5, Gdom7♭5)
G dominant seventh, flat fifth

G	B	D♭	F
root	3rd	♭5th	♭7th

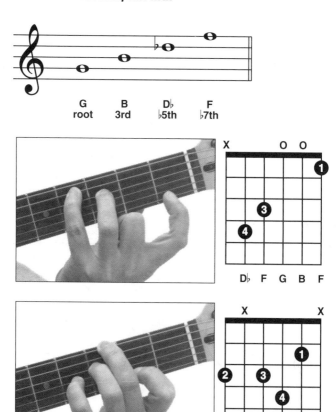

D♭ F G B F

G F B D♭

G9
G ninth

G	B	D	F	A
root	3rd	5th	♭7th	9th

G A D A B F

G B F A

4fr

G9sus4 (G9sus)

G ninth, suspended fourth

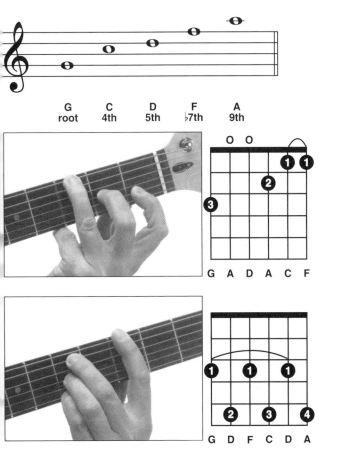

G	C	D	F	A
root	4th	5th	♭7th	9th

G A D A C F

G D F C D A

G9♭5 (G9-5, Gdom9♭5)

G ninth, flat fifth

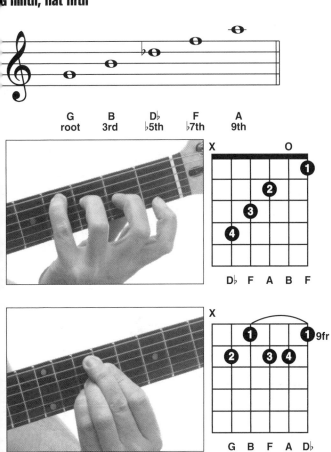

G	B	D♭	F	A
root	3rd	♭5th	♭7th	9th

D♭ F A B F

G B F A D♭

G

G7♭9 (G7-9, Gdom7♭9)
G dominant seventh, flat ninth

G	B	D	F	A♭
root	3rd	5th	♭7th	♭9th

G B D A♭ D F

G7♭9 — 6fr

B A♭ D F

G7♯9 (G7+9, Gdom7♯9)
G dominant seventh, sharp ninth

G	B	D	F	A♯
root	3rd	5th	♭7th	♯9th

G B D A♯ B F

G7♯9 — 4fr

G B F A♯

G7♭5(♯9) (G7-5(+9), Gdom7♭5(♯9))

dominant seventh, flat fifth, sharp ninth

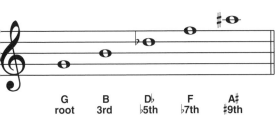

G	B	D♭	F	A♯
root	3rd	♭5th	♭7th	♯9th

B   A♯ D♭   F

G   B   F   A♯   D♭

G11

G eleventh

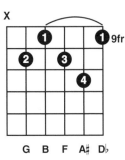

G	B	D	F	A	C
root	3rd	5th	♭7th	9th	11th

G B D A C F

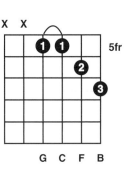

G C F B

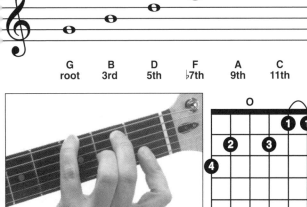

G

G7#11 (G7+11, Gdom7#11)
G dominant seventh, sharp eleventh

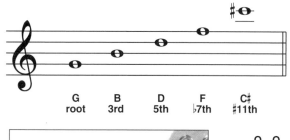

G root	B 3rd	D 5th	F ♭7th	C# #11th

G B D G C# F

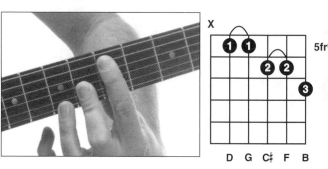

5fr

D G C# F B

G13 (Gdom13)
G thirteenth

G root	B 3rd	D 5th	F ♭7th	A 9th	E 13th

G A F A B E

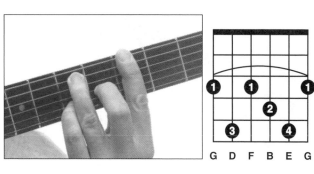

G D F B E G

G7♭5(♯9) (G7-5(+9), Gdom7♭5(♯9))

G dominant seventh, flat fifth, sharp ninth

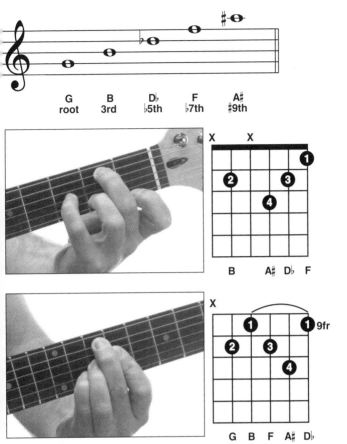

G	B	D♭	F	A♯
root	3rd	♭5th	♭7th	♯9th

B   A♯ D♭ F

G B F A♯ D♭ 9fr

G11

G eleventh

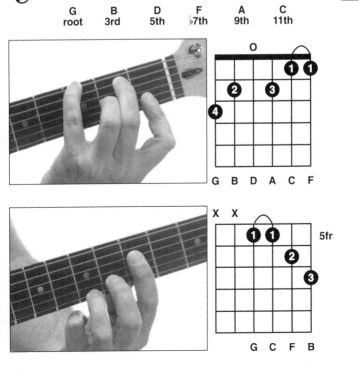

G	B	D	F	A	C
root	3rd	5th	♭7th	9th	11th

G B D A C F

G C F B 5fr

G

G7♯11 (G7+11, Gdom7♯11)
G dominant seventh, sharp eleventh

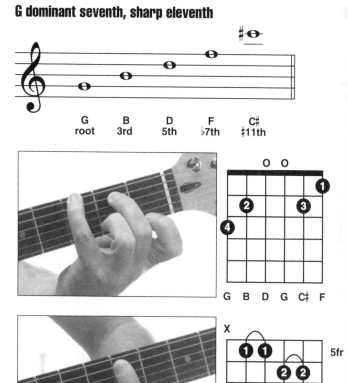

G	B	D	F	C♯
root	3rd	5th	♭7th	♯11th

G B D G C♯ F

X   5fr

D G C♯ F B

G13 (Gdom13)
G thirteenth

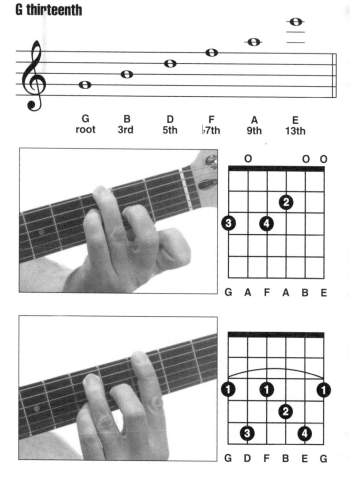

G	B	D	F	A	E
root	3rd	5th	♭7th	9th	13th

G A F A B E

G D F B E G

G13sus4 (G13sus)

G thirteenth, suspended fourth

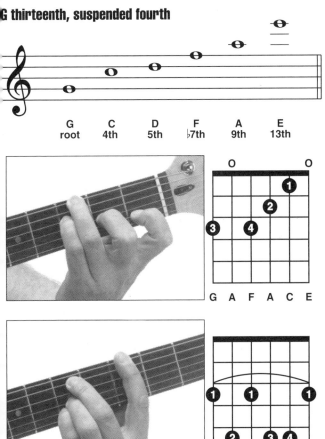

G	C	D	F	A	E
root	4th	5th	♭7th	9th	13th

G A F A C E

G D F C E G

G+ (Gaug, G(♯5))

G augmented

G	B	D♯
root	3rd	♯5th

G B D♯ G B G

G B D♯ G

8fr

G+7 (G7♯5)

G dominant seventh, sharp fifth

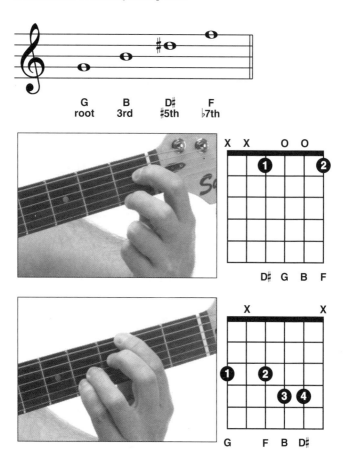

G	B	D♯	F
root	3rd	♯5th	♭7th

X X O O

❶ ❷

D♯ G B F

X X

❶ ❷

❸ ❹

G F B D♯

G° (Gdim)

G diminished

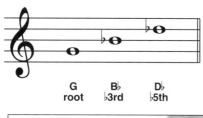

G	B♭	D♭
root	♭3rd	♭5th

X X O

❶

❷

❸

B♭ G D♭ G

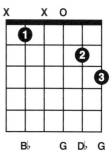

X X

❶ ❶ 6fr

❸ ❹

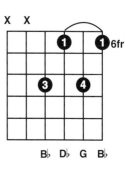

B♭ D♭ G B♭

G°7 (Gdim7)

G diminished seventh

G	B♭	D♭	F♭
root	♭3rd	♭5th	♭♭7th

A♭ (A♭maj)
A-flat major

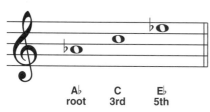

A♭	C	E♭
root	3rd	5th

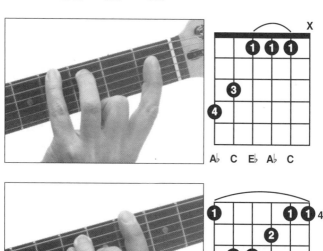

X

A♭ C E♭ A♭ C

4fr

A♭ E♭ A♭ C E♭ A♭

A♭5 (A♭(no3rd))
A-flat fifth (power chord)

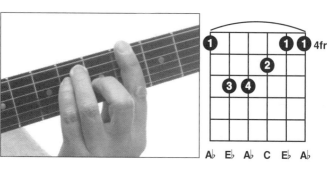

A♭	E♭
root	5th

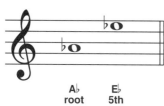

X X X

4fr

A♭ E♭ A♭

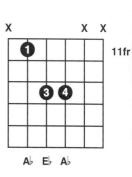

X X X

11fr

A♭ E♭ A♭

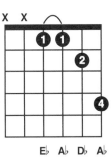

A♭sus4 (A♭sus)
A-flat suspended fourth

A♭	D♭	E♭
root	4th	5th

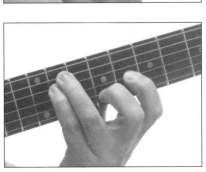

X X

E♭ A♭ D♭ A♭

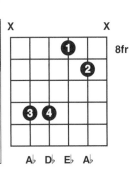

X   X

8fr

A♭ D♭ E♭ A♭

A♭sus2 (A♭5add2)
A-flat suspended second

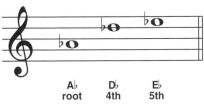

A♭	B♭	E♭
root	2nd	5th

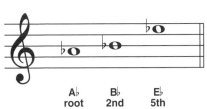

X X

6fr

A♭ E♭ A♭ B♭

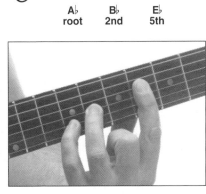

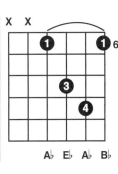

X   X

8fr

A♭ B♭ E♭ A♭

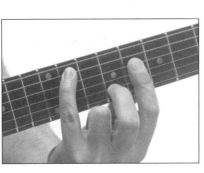

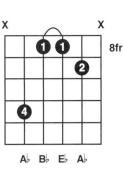

A♭

A♭add9
A-flat added ninth

A♭	C	E♭	B♭
root	3rd	5th	9th

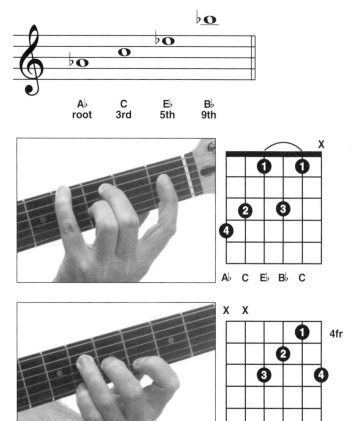

A♭ C E♭ B♭ C

A♭ C E♭ B♭

A♭6
A-flat sixth

A♭	C	E♭	F
root	3rd	5th	6th

A♭ C E♭ A♭ C F

A♭ F C E♭

A♭6/9 (A♭6add9)
A-flat sixth, added ninth

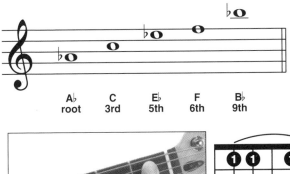

A♭	C	E♭	F	B♭
root	3rd	5th	6th	9th

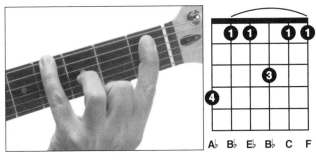

A♭ B♭ E♭ B♭ C F

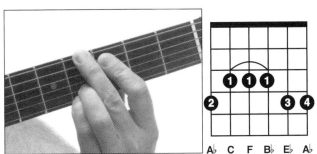

A♭ C F B♭ E♭ A♭

A♭maj7 (A♭M7)
A-flat major seventh

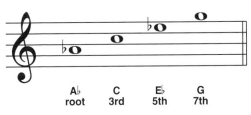

A♭	C	E♭	G
root	3rd	5th	7th

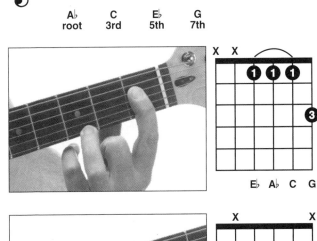

X X

E♭ A♭ C G

A♭

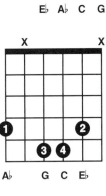

X X

A♭ G C E♭

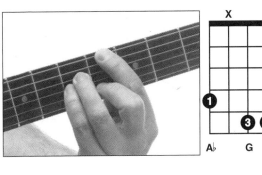

A♭maj9 (A♭M9)

A-flat major ninth

A♭	C	E♭	G	B♭
root	3rd	5th	7th	9th

A♭ B♭ E♭ B♭ C G

X   X
10fr

A♭ C G B♭

A♭maj7♯11 (A♭M7♯11)

A-flat major seventh, sharp eleventh

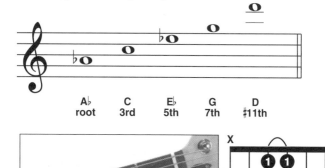

A♭	C	E♭	G	D
root	3rd	5th	7th	♯11th

X

C E♭ A♭ D G

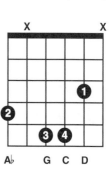

X   X

A♭ G C D

A♭maj13 (A♭M13)
A-flat major thirteenth

A♭	C	E♭	G	B♭	F
root	3rd	5th	7th	9th	13th

A♭ C F B♭ E♭ G

A♭ G C F 4fr

A♭m (A♭min, A♭-)
A-flat minor

A♭	C♭	E♭
root	♭3rd	5th

A♭ E♭ A♭ C♭ E♭ A♭ 4fr

A♭ E♭ A♭ C♭ E♭ 11fr

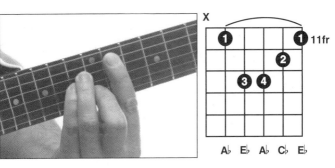

A♭

A♭m(add9)
A-flat minor, added ninth

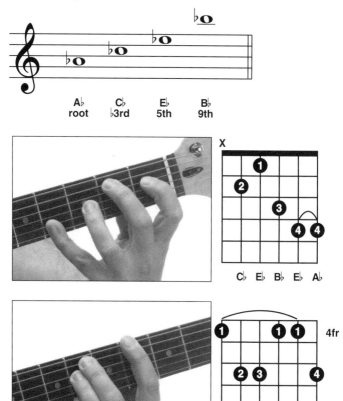

A♭	C♭	E♭	B♭
root	♭3rd	5th	9th

C♭ E♭ B♭ E♭ A♭

A♭ E♭ A♭ C♭ E♭ B♭　4fr

A♭m6　(A♭min6, A♭-6)
A-flat minor sixth

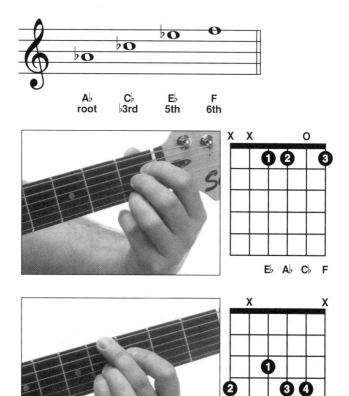

A♭	C♭	E♭	F
root	♭3rd	5th	6th

E♭ A♭ C♭ F

A♭ F C♭ E♭

A♭m♭6 (A♭-(♭6), A♭min♭6)
A-flat minor, flat sixth

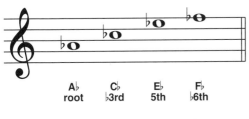

A♭	C♭	E♭	F♭
root	♭3rd	5th	♭6th

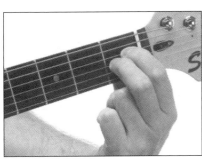

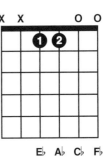

E♭ A♭ C♭ F♭

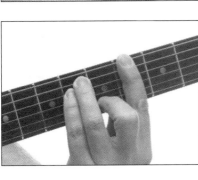

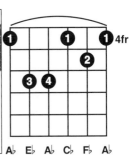 4fr

A♭ E♭ A♭ C♭ F♭ A♭

A♭m6/9
A-flat minor sixth, added ninth

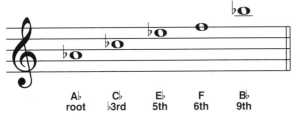

A♭	C♭	E♭	F	B♭
root	♭3rd	5th	6th	9th

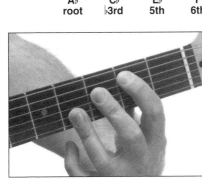

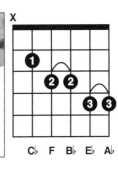

C♭ F B♭ E♭ A♭

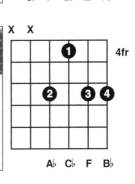 4fr

A♭ C♭ F B♭

A♭

A♭m7 (A♭-7, A♭min7)

A-flat minor seventh

A♭	C♭	E♭	G♭
root	♭3rd	5th	♭7th

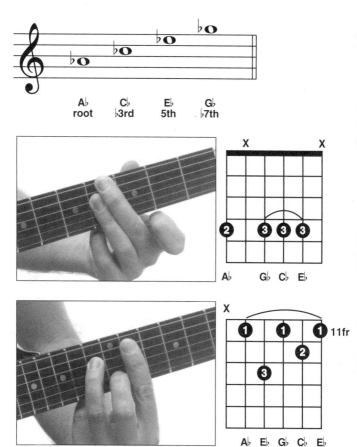

A♭m7♭5 (A♭-7♭5, A♭min7-5)

A-flat minor seventh, flat fifth

A♭	C♭	E♭♭	G♭
root	♭3rd	♭5th	♭7th

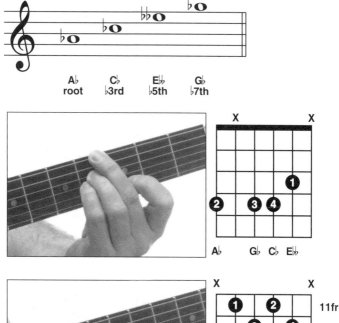

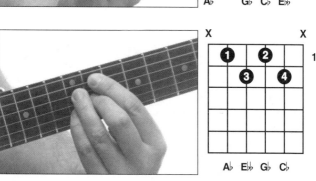

A♭m(maj7) (A♭-(+7))

A-flat minor, major seventh

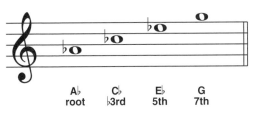

A♭	C♭	E♭	G
root	♭3rd	5th	7th

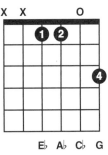

E♭ A♭ C♭ G

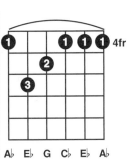

4fr

A♭ E♭ G C♭ E♭ A♭

A♭m9 (A♭-9, A♭min9)

A-flat minor ninth

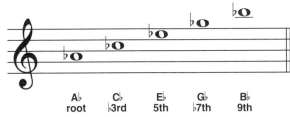

A♭	C♭	E♭	G♭	B♭
root	♭3rd	5th	♭7th	9th

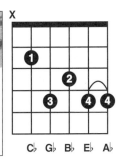

C♭ G♭ B♭ E♭ A♭

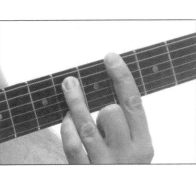
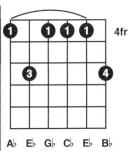

4fr

A♭ E♭ G♭ C♭ E♭ B♭

A♭

A♭m9♭5 (A♭m9-5, A♭min9♭5)
A-flat minor ninth, flat fifth

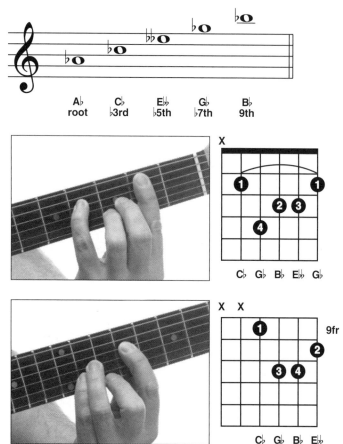

A♭	C♭	E♭♭	G♭	B♭
root	♭3rd	♭5th	♭7th	9th

X

C♭ G♭ B♭ E♭ G♭

X X 9fr

C♭ G♭ B♭ E♭

A♭m9(maj7) (A♭m9+7, A♭-9+7)
A-flat minor ninth, major seventh

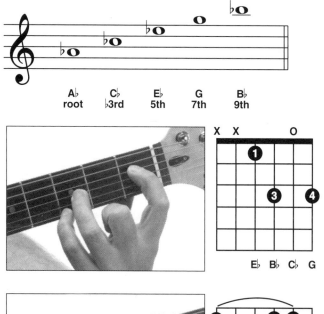

A♭	C♭	E♭	G	B♭
root	♭3rd	5th	7th	9th

X X O

E♭ B♭ C♭ G

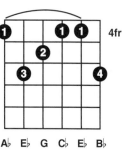

4fr

A♭ E♭ G C♭ E♭ B♭

A♭m11 (A♭-11, A♭min11)
A-flat minor eleventh

A♭	C♭	E♭	G♭	B♭	D♭
root	♭3rd	5th	♭7th	9th	11th

A♭m13 (A♭-13, A♭min13)
A-flat minor thirteenth

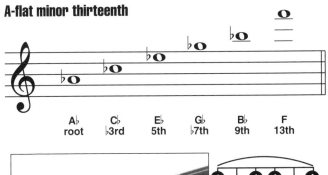

A♭	C♭	E♭	G♭	B♭	F
root	♭3rd	5th	♭7th	9th	13th

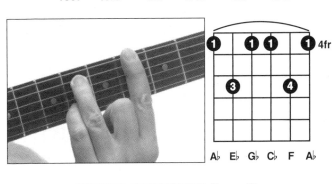

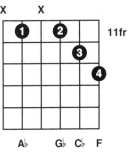

A♭7 (A♭dom7)

A-flat dominant seventh

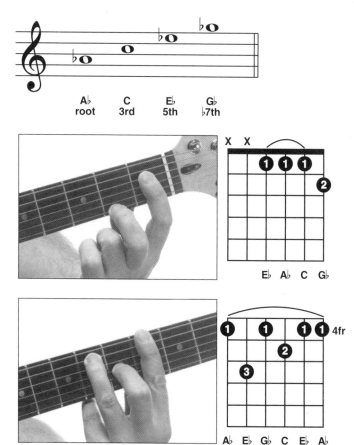

A♭	C	E♭	G♭
root	3rd	5th	♭7th

E♭ A♭ C G♭

A♭ E♭ G♭ C E♭ A♭

A♭7sus4 (A♭7sus)

A-flat dominant seventh, suspended fourth

A♭	D♭	E♭	G♭
root	4th	5th	♭7th

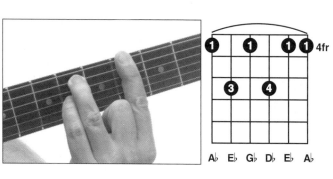

E♭ A♭ D♭ G♭

A♭ E♭ G♭ D♭ E♭ A♭

A♭7♭5 (A♭7-5, A♭dom7♭5)

A-flat dominant seventh, flat fifth

A♭	C	E♭♭	G♭
root	3rd	♭5th	♭7th

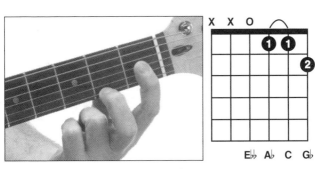

X X O

E♭♭ A♭ C G♭

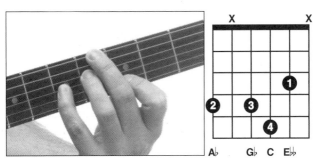

X X

A♭ G♭ C E♭♭

A♭9

A-flat ninth

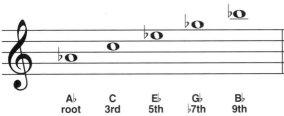

A♭	C	E♭	G♭	B♭
root	3rd	5th	♭7th	9th

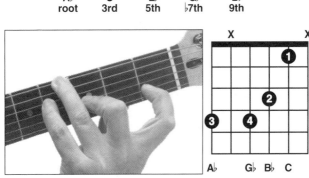

X X

A♭ G♭ B♭ C

A♭

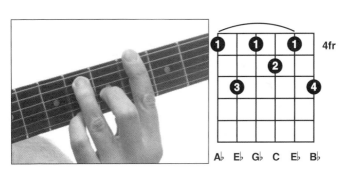

4fr

A♭ E♭ G♭ C E♭ B♭

A♭9sus4 (A♭9sus)
A-flat ninth, suspended fourth

A♭	D♭	E♭	G♭	B♭
root	4th	5th	♭7th	9th

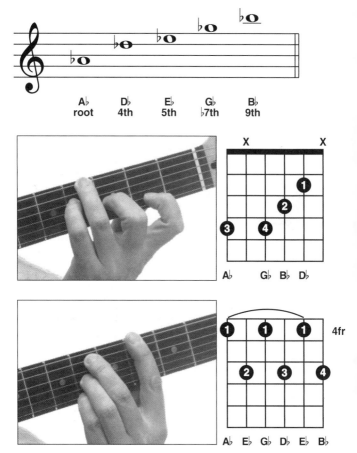

A♭ G♭ B♭ D♭

A♭ E♭ G♭ D♭ E♭ B♭ 4fr

A♭9♭5 (A♭9-5, A♭dom9♭5)
A-flat ninth, flat fifth

A♭	C	E♭♭	G♭	B♭
root	3rd	♭5th	♭7th	9th

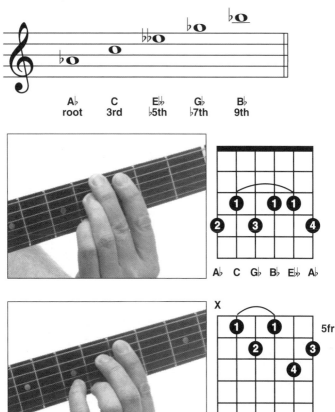

A♭ C G♭ B♭ E♭♭ A♭

E♭♭ A♭ C G♭ B♭ 5fr

A♭7♭9 (A♭7-9, A♭dom7♭9)
A-flat dominant seventh, flat ninth

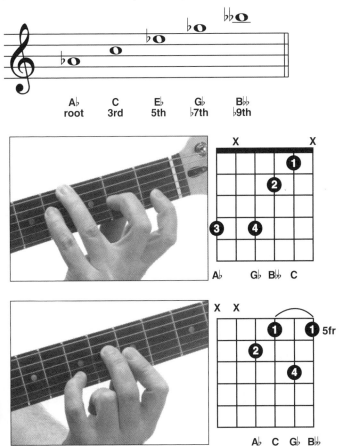

A♭	C	E♭	G♭	B♭♭
root	3rd	5th	♭7th	♭9th

A♭   G♭ B♭♭ C

A♭ C G♭ B♭♭

A♭7♯9 (A♭7+9, A♭dom7♯9)
A-flat dominant seventh, sharp ninth

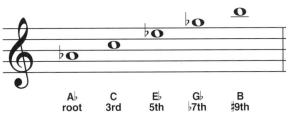

A♭	C	E♭	G♭	B
root	3rd	5th	♭7th	♯9th

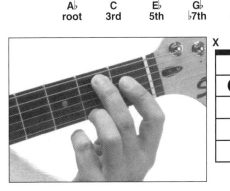

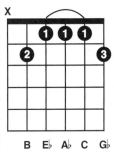

B E♭ A♭ C G♭

A♭

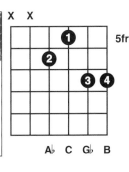

A♭ C G♭ B

A♭7♭5(♯9) <small>(A♭7-5(+9), A♭dom7♭5(♯9))</small>

A-flat dominant seventh, flat fifth, sharp ninth

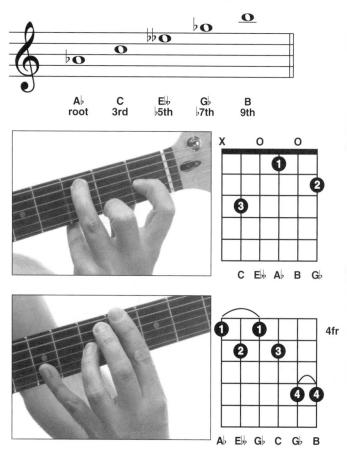

A♭	C	E♭♭	G♭	B
root	3rd	♭5th	♭7th	9th

X O O

C E♭♭ A♭ B G♭

4fr

A♭ E♭♭ G♭ C G♭ B

A♭11

A-flat eleventh

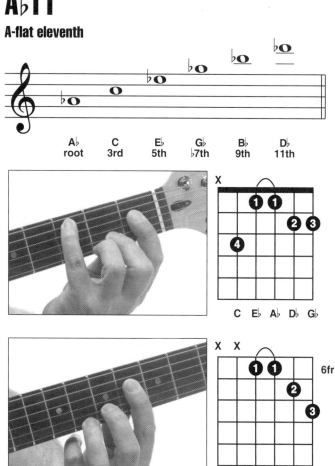

A♭	C	E♭	G♭	B♭	D♭
root	3rd	5th	♭7th	9th	11th

X

C E♭ A♭ D♭ G♭

X X

6fr

A♭ D♭ G♭ C

A♭7♯11 (A♭7+11, A♭dom7♯11)
A-flat dominant seventh, sharp eleventh

A♭	C	E♭	G♭	D
root	3rd	5th	♭7th	♯11th

X X O

1 1
2

D A♭ C G♭

X

1   1   9fr
2   3
4

G♭ C G♭ A♭ D

A♭13 (A♭dom13)
A-flat thirteenth

A♭	C	E♭	G♭	B♭	F
root	3rd	5th	♭7th	9th	13th

1 1 1 1 1
2

G♭ B♭ E♭ A♭ C F

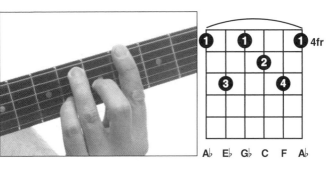

1   1   1   4fr
2
3   4

A♭ E♭ G♭ C F A♭

A♭

A♭13sus4 (A♭13sus)
A-flat thirteenth, suspended fourth

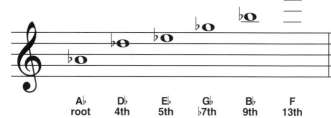

A♭	D♭	E♭	G♭	B♭	F
root	4th	5th	♭7th	9th	13th

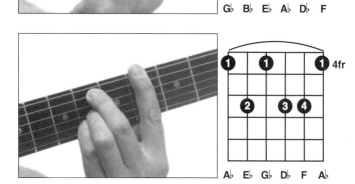

G♭ B♭ E♭ A♭ D♭ F

4fr

A♭ E♭ G♭ D♭ F A♭

A♭+ (A♭aug, A♭(♯5))
A-flat augmented

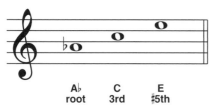

A♭	C	E
root	3rd	♯5th

E C E A♭ C E

9fr

A♭ C E A♭

A♭+7   (A♭7♯5)

A-flat dominant seventh, sharp fifth

A♭	C	E	G♭
root	3rd	♯5th	♭7th

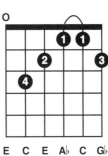

E C E A♭ C G♭

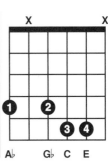

A♭   G♭ C E

A♭°   (A♭dim)

A-flat diminished

A♭	C♭	E♭♭
root	♭3rd	♭5th

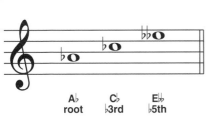

C♭ E♭♭ A♭ E♭♭ A♭

A♭

A♭   C♭ E♭♭ A♭

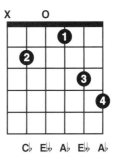

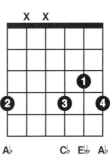

A♭°7 (A♭dim7)
A-flat diminished seventh

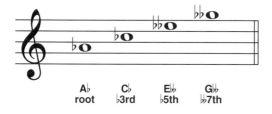

A♭	C♭	E♭♭	G♭♭
root	♭3rd	♭5th	♭♭7th

X X O O

E♭♭ A♭ C♭ G♭♭

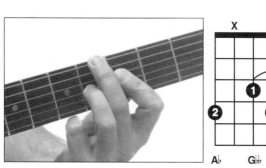

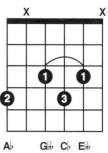

X X

A♭ G♭♭ C♭ E♭♭

A (Amaj)
A major

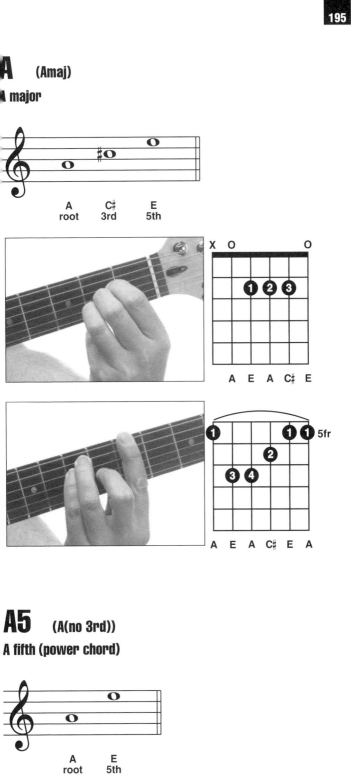

A — root
C# — 3rd
E — 5th

X O   O

1 2 3

A E A C# E

1   1 1 5fr
2
3 4

A E A C# E A

A5 (A(no 3rd))
A fifth (power chord)

A — root
E — 5th

X O   X X

1 1

A E A

X O

1 1

4 4

A E A E A

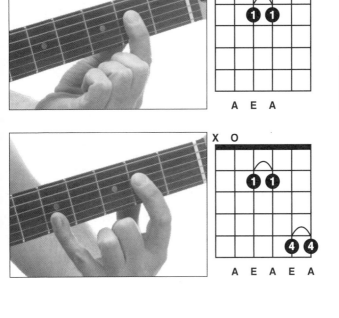

Asus4 (Asus)

A suspended fourth

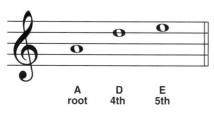

A   D   E
root   4th   5th

A E A D E

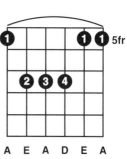

A E A D E A

Asus2 (A5add2)

A suspended second

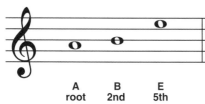

A   B   E
root   2nd   5th

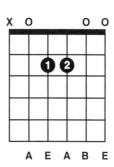

A E A B E

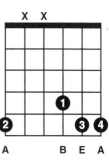

A   B E A

Aadd9

A added ninth

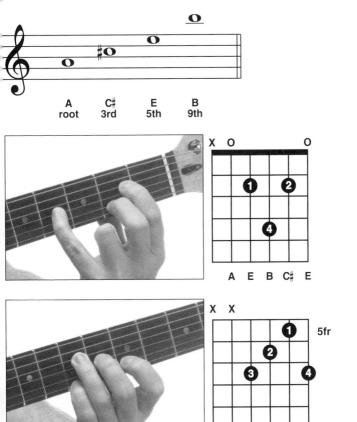

A	C#	E	B
root	3rd	5th	9th

X O   O

A E B C# E

X X   5fr

A C# E B

A6

A sixth

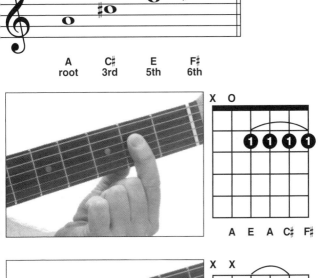

A	C#	E	F#
root	3rd	5th	6th

X O

A E A C# F#

A

X X   7fr

A E F# C#

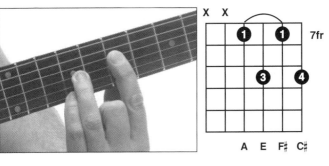

A6/9 (A6add9)
A sixth, added ninth

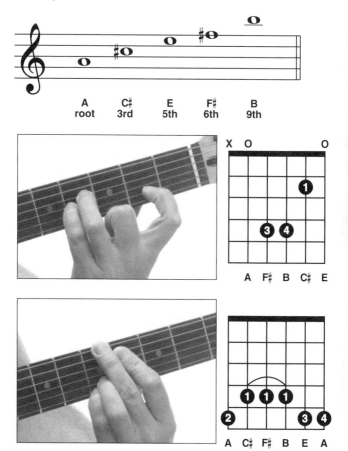

A	C#	E	F#	B
root	3rd	5th	6th	9th

A F# B C# E

A C# F# B E A

Amaj7 (AM7)
A major seventh

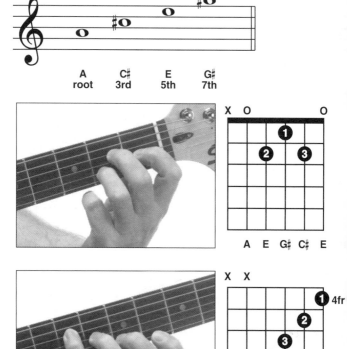

A	C#	E	G#
root	3rd	5th	7th

A E G# C# E

A C# E G#

Amaj9 (AM9)
major ninth

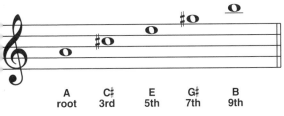

A	C#	E	G#	B
root	3rd	5th	7th	9th

X O

A E B C# G#

X X

6fr

A C# G# B

Amaj7#11 (AM7#11)
A major seventh, sharp eleventh

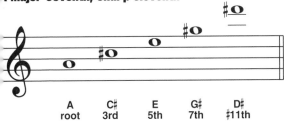

A	C#	E	G#	D#
root	3rd	5th	7th	#11th

X O   O

A D# G# C# E

X

C# E A D# G#

A

Amaj13 (AM13)

A major thirteenth

A	C#	E	G#	B	F#
root	3rd	5th	7th	9th	13th

A E G# C# F#

A C# F# B E G#

Am (Amin, A-)

A minor

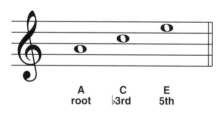

A	C	E
root	♭3rd	5th

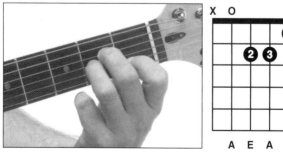

A E A C E

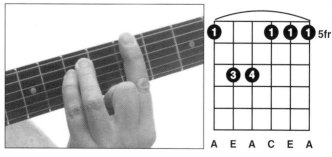

A E A C E A

Am(add9)

A minor, added ninth

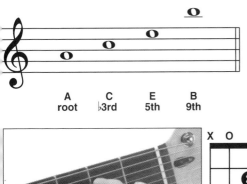

A	C	E	B
root	♭3rd	5th	9th

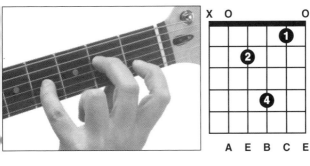

Am6 (Amin6, A-6)

A minor sixth

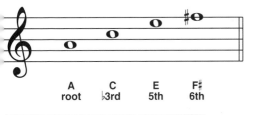

A	C	E	F♯
root	♭3rd	5th	6th

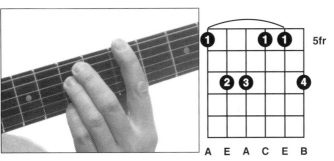

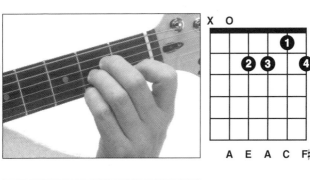

A

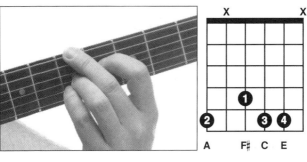

Am♭6 (A-(♭6), Amin♭6)

A minor, flat sixth

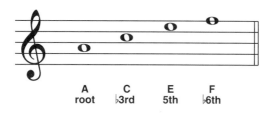

A	C	E	F
root	♭3rd	5th	♭6th

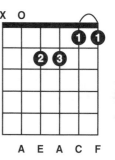

A E A C F

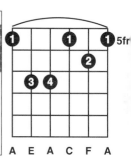

5fr

A E A C F A

Am6/9

A minor sixth, added ninth

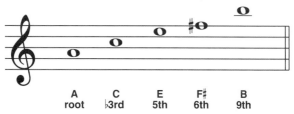

A	C	E	F♯	B
root	♭3rd	5th	6th	9th

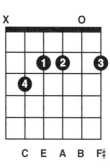

C E A B F♯

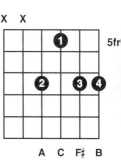

5fr

A C F♯ B

Am7 (A-7, Amin7)

A minor seventh

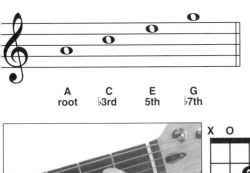

A	C	E	G
root	♭3rd	5th	♭7th

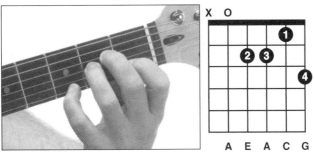

X O

A E A C G

A E G C E A · 5fr

Am7♭5 (A-7♭5, Amin7♭5)

A minor seventh, flat fifth

A	C	E♭	G
root	♭3rd	♭5th	♭7th

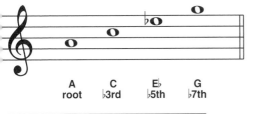

X O

A E♭ A C G

A

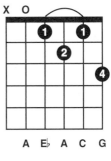

X X

A G C E♭

Am(maj7) (A-(+7))

A minor, major seventh

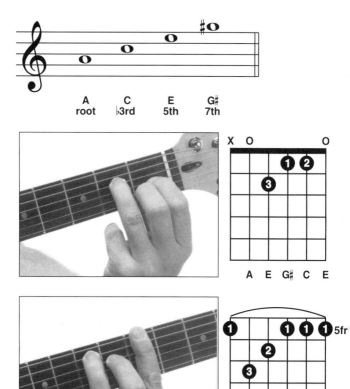

A	C	E	G#
root	♭3rd	5th	7th

A E G# C E

A E G# C E A

Am9 (A-9, Amin9)

A minor ninth

A	C	E	G	B
root	♭3rd	5th	♭7th	9th

A C E G B E

A C G B

Am9♭5 (Am9-5, Amin9♭5)

A minor ninth, flat fifth

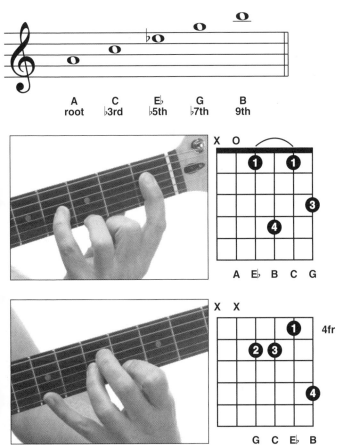

A	C	E♭	G	B
root	♭3rd	♭5th	♭7th	9th

A E♭ B C G

G C E♭ B

Am9(maj7) (Am9+7, A-9+7)

A minor ninth, major seventh

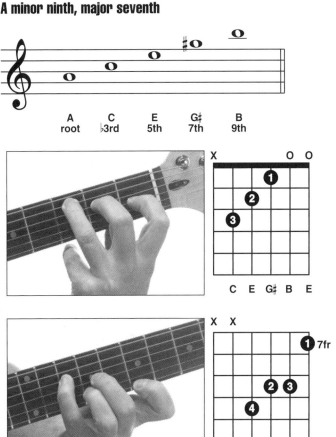

A	C	E	G#	B
root	♭3rd	5th	7th	9th

C E G# B E

C E G# B

A

Am11 (A-11, Amin11)
A minor eleventh

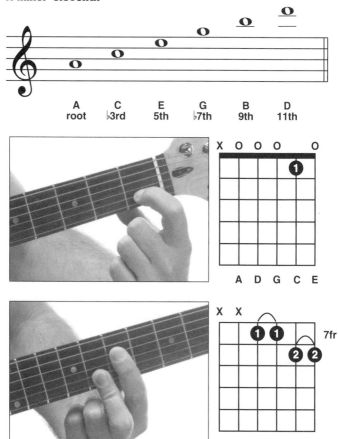

A	C	E	G	B	D
root	♭3rd	5th	♭7th	9th	11th

Am13 (A-13, Amin13)
A minor thirteenth

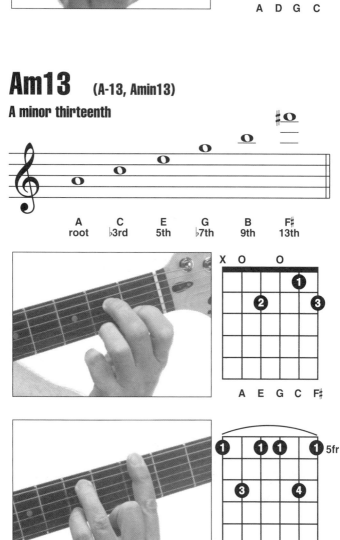

A	C	E	G	B	F♯
root	♭3rd	5th	♭7th	9th	13th

A7 (Adom7)

A dominant seventh

A root	C# 3rd	E 5th	♭7th G

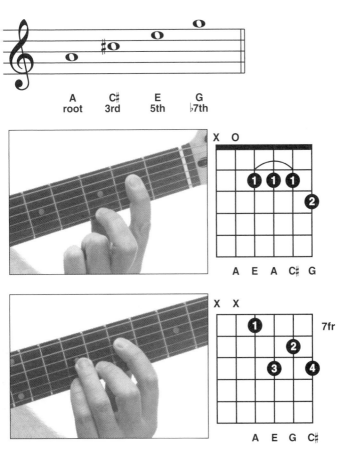

X O

A E A C# G

X X

7fr

A E G C#

A7sus4 (A7sus)

A dominant seventh, suspended fourth

A root	D 4th	E 5th	♭7th G

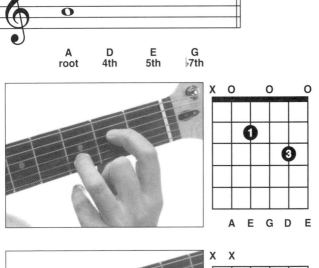

X O O O

A E G D E

A

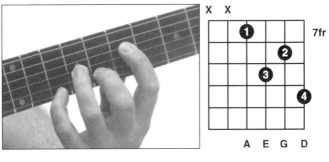

X X

7fr

A E G D

A7♭5 (A7-5, Adom7♭5)
A dominant seventh, flat fifth

A	C#	E♭	G
root	3rd	♭5th	♭7th

A9
A ninth

A	C#	E	G	B
root	3rd	5th	♭7th	9th

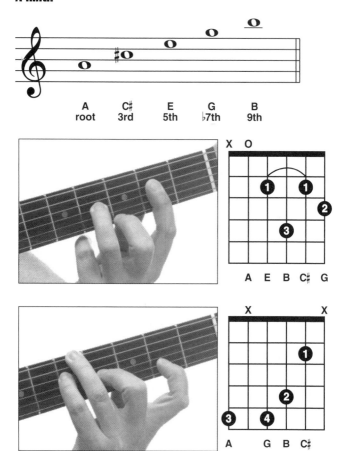

A9sus4 (A9sus)
A ninth, suspended fourth

A	D	E	G	B
root	4th	5th	7th	9th

A E B D G

A G B D

A7♭9 (A7-9, Adom7♭9)
A dominant seventh, flat ninth

A	C#	E	G	B♭
root	3rd	5th	♭7th	♭9th

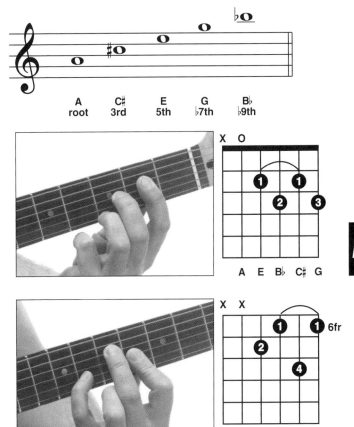

A E B♭ C# G

A C# G B♭

6fr

A

A7#9 (A7+9, Adom7#9)
A dominant seventh, sharp ninth

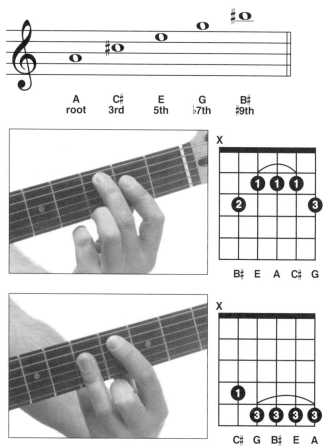

A	C#	E	G	B#
root	3rd	5th	b7th	#9th

X

B# E A C# G

X

C# G B# E A

A7b5(#9) (A7-5(+9), Adom7b5(#9))
A dominant seventh, flat fifth, sharp ninth

A	C#	Eb	G	B#
root	3rd	b5th	b7th	#9th

X   O

B# Eb G C# G

5fr

A Eb G C# G B#

A11
A eleventh

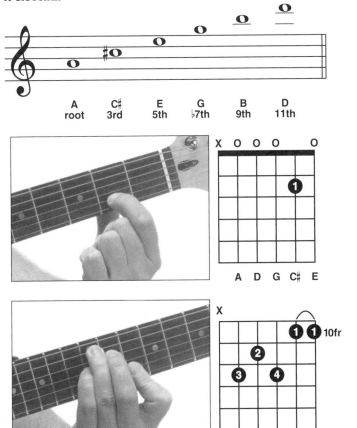

A	C#	E	G	B	D
root	3rd	5th	♭7th	9th	11th

X O O O   O

A D G C# E

X   10fr

A C# G A D

A7#11 (A7+11, Adom7#11)
A dominant seventh, sharp eleventh

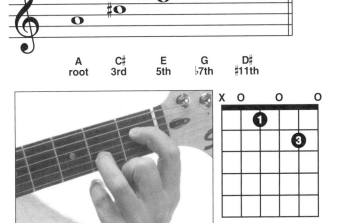

A	C#	E	G	D#
root	3rd	5th	♭7th	#11th

X O O O

A D# G C# E

X   X   4fr

A G C# D#

A

A13 (Adom13)
A thirteenth

A	C#	E	G	B	F#
root	3rd	5th	♭7th	9th	13th

X O O

A E G C# F#

5fr

A E G C# F# A

A13sus4 (A13sus)
A thirteenth, suspended fourth

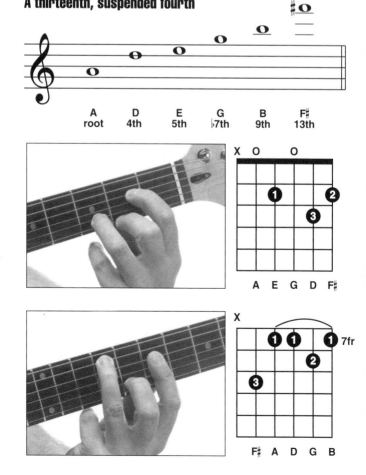

A	D	E	G	B	F#
root	4th	5th	♭7th	9th	13th

X O O

A E G D F#

7fr

X

F# A D G B

A+ (Aaug, A(♯5))
A augmented

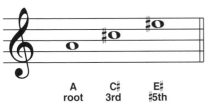

A	C♯	E♯
root	3rd	♯5th

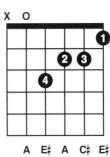

A E♯ A C♯ E♯

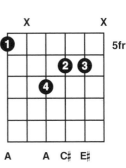

5fr

A A C♯ E♯

A+7 (A7♯5)
A dominant seventh, sharp fifth

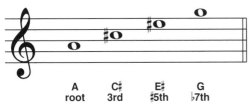

A	C♯	E♯	G
root	3rd	♯5th	♭7th

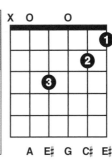

A E♯ G C♯ E♯

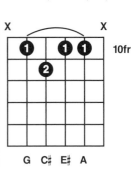

10fr

G C♯ E♯ A

A° (Adim)
A diminished

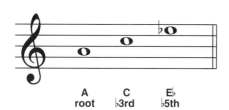

A	C	E♭
root	♭3rd	♭5th

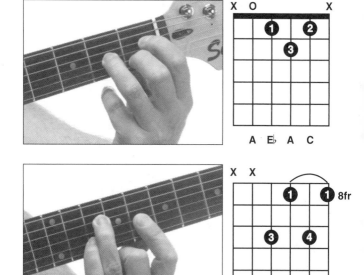

A E♭ A C

C E♭ A C

A°7 (Adim7)
A diminished seventh

A	C	E♭	G♭♭
root	♭3rd	♭5th	♭♭7th

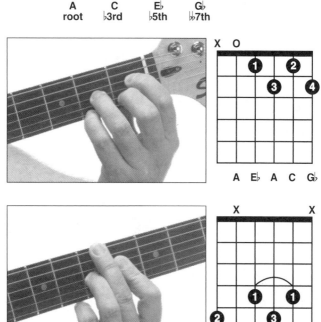

A E♭ A C G♭

A G♭ C E♭

B♭ (B♭maj)
B-flat major

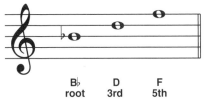

B♭	D	F
root	3rd	5th

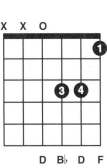

D B♭ D F

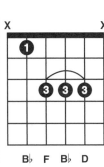

B♭ F B♭ D

B♭5 (B♭(no 3rd))
B-flat fifth (power chord)

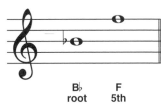

B♭	F
root	5th

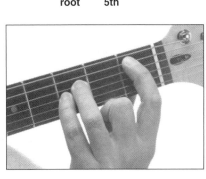
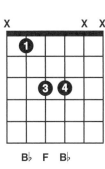

B♭ F B♭

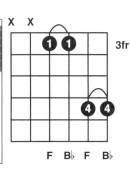

3fr

F B♭ F B♭

B♭sus4 (B♭sus)

B-flat suspended fourth

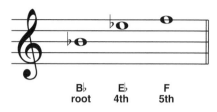

B♭	E♭	F
root	4th	5th

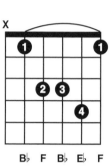

B♭ F B♭ E♭ F

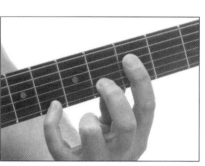

3fr

F B♭ E♭ B♭

B♭sus2 (B♭5add2)

B-flat suspended second

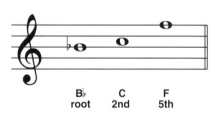

B♭	C	F
root	2nd	5th

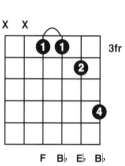

B♭ F B♭ C F

5fr

B♭ C F B♭

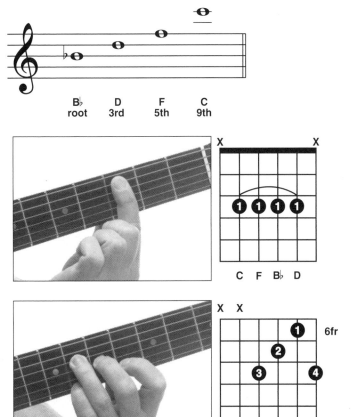

B♭add9
B-flat added ninth

B♭	D	F	C
root	3rd	5th	9th

C F B♭ D

B♭ D F C 6fr

B♭6
B-flat sixth

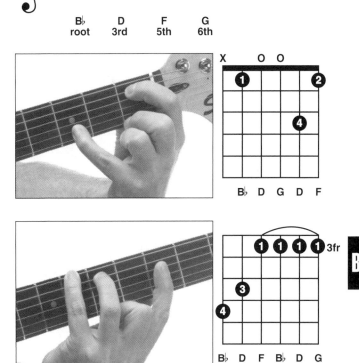

B♭	D	F	G
root	3rd	5th	6th

B♭ D G D F

B♭ D F B♭ D G 3fr

B♭

B♭6/9 (B♭6add9)
B-flat sixth, added ninth

B♭	D	F	G	C
root	3rd	5th	6th	9th

B♭ D G C F

B♭ C F B♭ D G

B♭maj7 (B♭M7)
B-flat major seventh

B♭	D	F	A
root	3rd	5th	7th

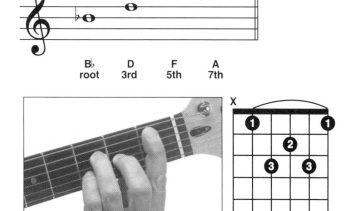

B♭ F A D F

B♭ D F A

B♭maj9 (B♭M9)
B-flat major ninth

B♭	D	F	A	C
root	3rd	5th	7th	9th

B♭ D A C F

B♭ D A C
7fr

B♭maj7♯11 (B♭M7♯11)
B-flat major seventh, sharp eleventh

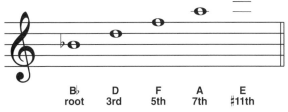

B♭	D	F	A	E
root	3rd	5th	7th	♯11th

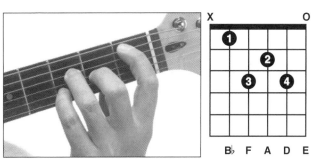

B♭ F A D E

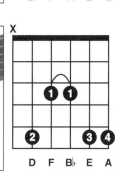

D F B♭ E A

B♭

B♭maj13 (B♭M13)
B-flat major thirteenth

B♭	D	F	A	C	G
root	3rd	5th	7th	9th	13th

B♭ F A D G

B♭ D G A D 10fr

B♭m (B♭min, B♭-)
B-flat minor

B♭	D♭	F
root	♭3rd	5th

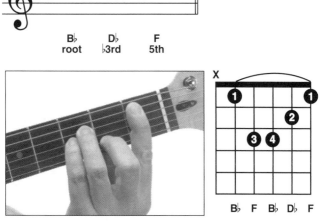

B♭ F B♭ D♭ F

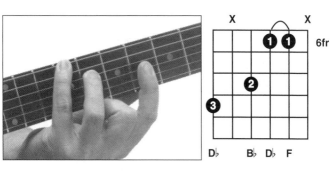

D♭ B♭ D♭ F 6fr

B♭m(add9)

B-flat minor, added ninth

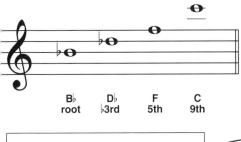
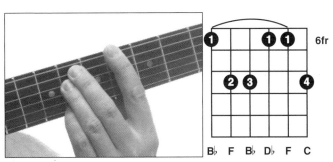

B♭	D♭	F	C
root	♭3rd	5th	9th

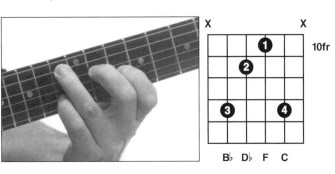

6fr

B♭ F B♭ D♭ F C

X · · · · X

10fr

B♭ D♭ F C

B♭m6 (B♭min6, B♭-6)

B-flat minor sixth

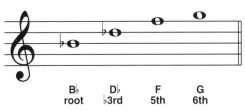

B♭	D♭	F	G
root	♭3rd	5th	6th

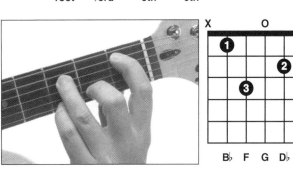

X · · O

B♭ F G D♭ G

X X

8fr

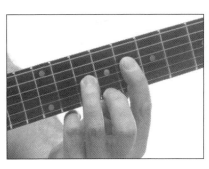
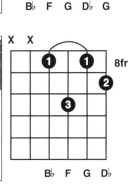

B♭ F G D♭

B♭

B♭m♭6 <small>(B♭-(♭6), B♭min♭6)</small>
B-flat minor, flat sixth

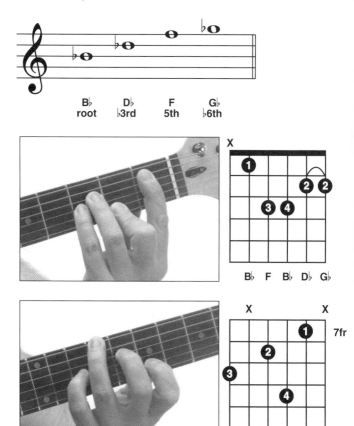

B♭	D♭	F	G♭
root	♭3rd	5th	♭6th

B♭ F B♭ D♭ G♭

D♭ B♭ F G♭

B♭m6/9
B-flat minor sixth, added ninth

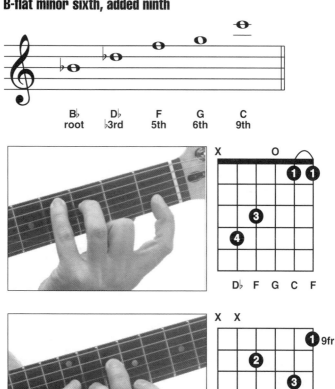

B♭	D♭	F	G	C
root	♭3rd	5th	6th	9th

D♭ F G C F

C G B♭ D♭

B♭m7 (B♭-7, B♭min7)
B-flat minor seventh

B♭	D♭	F	A♭
root	♭3rd	5th	♭7th

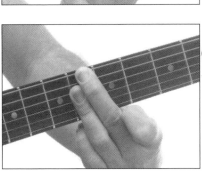

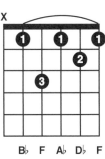

B♭ F A♭ D♭ F

B♭ A♭ D♭ F

6fr

B♭m7♭5 (B♭-7♭5, B♭min7♭5)
B-flat minor seventh, flat fifth

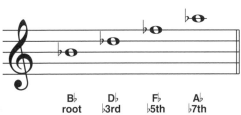

B♭	D♭	F♭	A♭
root	♭3rd	♭5th	♭7th

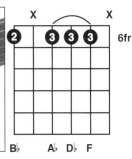

B♭ F♭ A♭ D♭ F♭

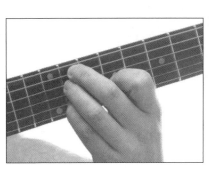

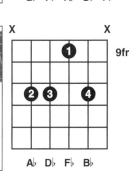

9fr

A♭ D♭ F♭ B♭

B♭

B♭m(maj7) (B♭-(+7))
B-flat minor, major seventh

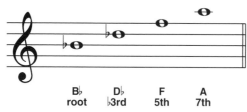

B♭	D♭	F	A
root	♭3rd	5th	7th

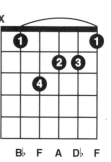

B♭ F A D♭ F

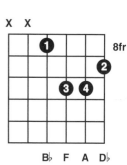

8fr

B♭ F A D♭

B♭m9 (B♭-9, B♭min9)
B-flat minor ninth

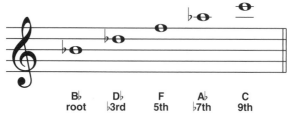

B♭	D♭	F	A♭	C
root	♭3rd	5th	♭7th	9th

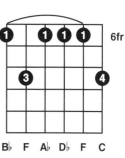

6fr

B♭ F A♭ D♭ F C

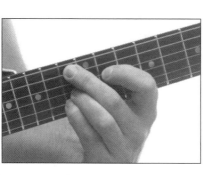
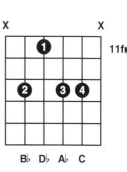

11fr

B♭ D♭ A♭ C

B♭m9♭5 (B♭m9-5, B♭minor9♭5)
B-flat minor ninth, flat fifth

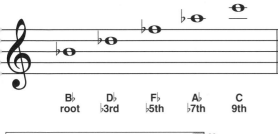

B♭	D♭	F♭	A♭	C
root	♭3rd	♭5th	♭7th	9th

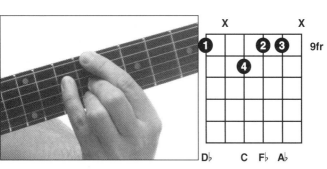

B♭m9(maj7) (B♭m9+7, B♭-9+7)
B-flat minor ninth, major seventh

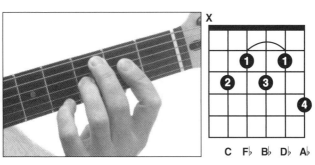

B♭	D♭	F	A	C
root	♭3rd	5th	7th	9th

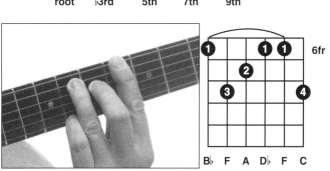

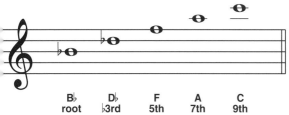

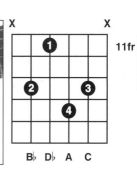

B♭m11 (B♭-11, B♭min11)

B-flat minor eleventh

B♭	D♭	F	A♭	C	E♭
root	♭3rd	5th	♭7th	9th	11th

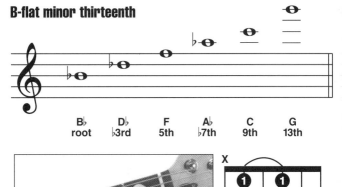

B♭m13 (B♭-13, B♭min13)

B-flat minor thirteenth

B♭	D♭	F	A♭	C	G
root	♭3rd	5th	♭7th	9th	13th

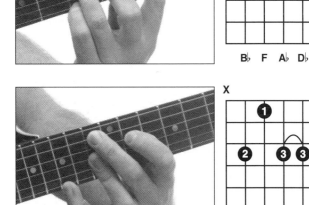

B♭7 (B♭dom7)

B-flat dominant seventh

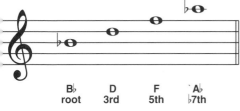

B♭	D	F	A♭
root	3rd	5th	♭7th

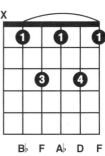

B♭ F A♭ D F

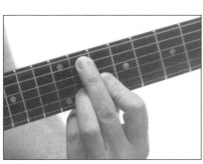
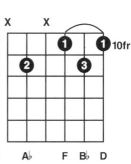

10fr

A♭ F B♭ D

B♭7sus4 (B♭7sus)

B-flat dominant seventh, suspended fourth

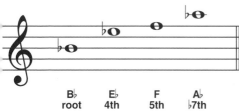

B♭	E♭	F	A♭
root	4th	5th	♭7th

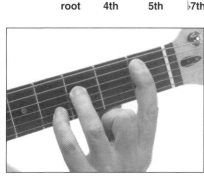
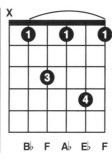

B♭ F A♭ E♭ F

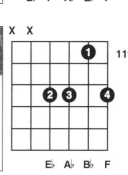

11fr

B♭

E♭ A♭ B♭ F

B♭7♭5 (B♭7-5, B♭dom7♭5)

B-flat dominant seventh, flat fifth

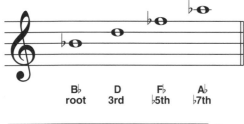

B♭	D	F♭	A♭
root	3rd	♭5th	♭7th

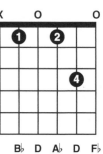

B♭ D A♭ D F♭

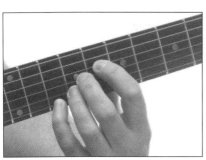
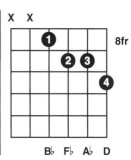

8fr

B♭ F♭ A♭ D

B♭9

B-flat ninth

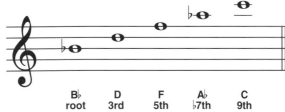

B♭	D	F	A♭	C
root	3rd	5th	♭7th	9th

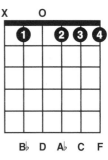

B♭ D A♭ C F

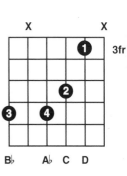

3fr

B♭ A♭ C D

B♭9sus4 (B♭9sus)

B-flat ninth, suspended fourth

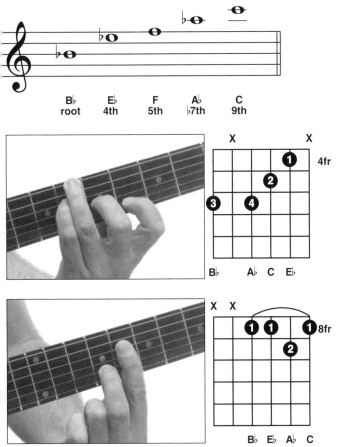

B♭	E♭	F	A♭	C
root	4th	5th	♭7th	9th

B♭7♭9 (B♭7-9, B♭dom7♭9)

B-flat dominant seventh, flat ninth

B♭	D	F	A♭	C♭
root	3rd	5th	♭7th	♭9th

B♭

B♭7♯9 (B♭7+9, B♭dom7♯9)
B-flat dominant seventh, sharp ninth

B♭	D	F	A♭	C♯
root	3rd	5th	♭7th	♯9th

B♭7♭5(♯9) (B♭7-5(+9), B♭dom7♭5(♯9))
B-flat dominant seventh, flat fifth, sharp ninth

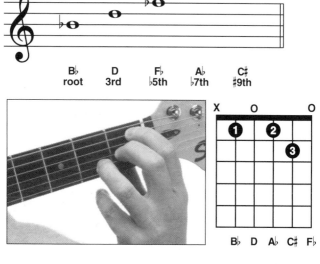

B♭	D	F♭	A♭	C♯
root	3rd	♭5th	♭7th	♯9th

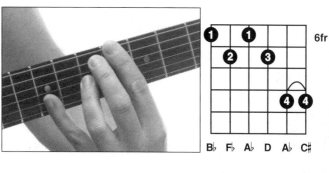

B♭11

B-flat eleventh

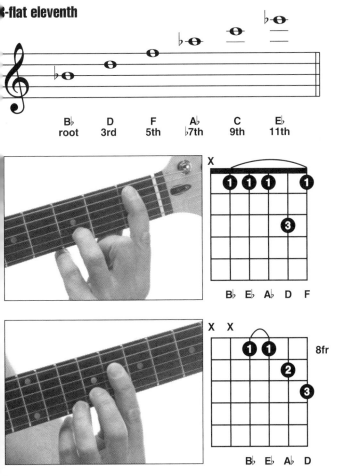

B♭	D	F	A♭	C	E♭
root	3rd	5th	♭7th	9th	11th

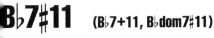

B♭ E♭ A♭ D F

8fr

B♭ E♭ A♭ D

B♭7♯11 (B♭7+11, B♭dom7♯11)

B-flat dominant seventh, sharp eleventh

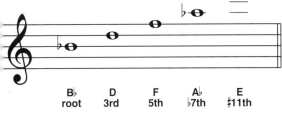

B♭	D	F	A♭	E
root	3rd	5th	♭7th	♯11th

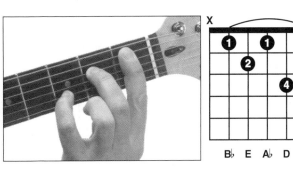

B♭ E A♭ D F

8fr

D B♭ E A♭

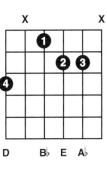

B♭

B♭13 (B♭dom13)

B-flat thirteenth

B♭	D	F	A♭	C	G
root	3rd	5th	♭7th	9th	13th

B♭ F A♭ D G

A♭ D G B♭

11

B♭13sus4 (B♭13sus)

B-flat thirteenth, suspended fourth

B♭	E♭	F	A♭	C	G
root	4th	5th	♭7th	9th	13th

B♭ E♭ A♭ C G

G B♭ E♭ A♭ C

8fr

B♭+ (B♭aug, B♭(♯5))

B-flat augmented

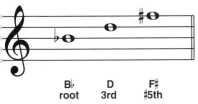

B♭	D	F♯
root	3rd	♯5th

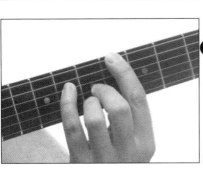

X   O

| B♭ | D | B♭ | D | F♯ |

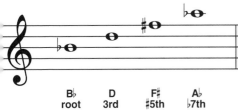

X   X

6fr

| B♭ | | B♭ | D | F♯ |

B♭+7 (B♭7♯5)

B-flat dominant seventh, sharp fifth

B♭	D	F♯	A♭
root	3rd	♯5th	♭7th

X   O

| B♭ | D | A♭ | D | F♯ |

X   X

11fr

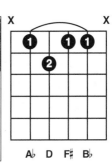

| A♭ | D | F♯ | B♭ |

B♭

B♭° (B♭dim)
B-flat diminshed

B♭	D♭	F♭
root	♭3rd	♭5th

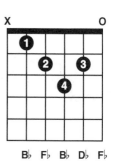

B♭ F♭ B♭ D♭ F♭

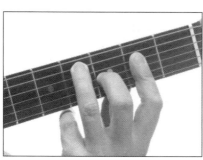

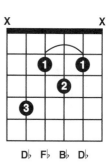

D♭ F♭ B♭ D♭

B♭°7 (B♭dim7)
B-flat diminished seventh

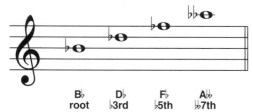

B♭	D♭	F♭	A♭♭
root	♭3rd	♭5th	♭♭7th

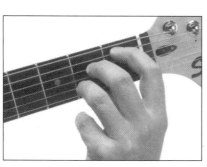

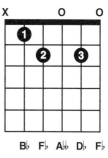

B♭ F♭ A♭♭ D♭ F♭

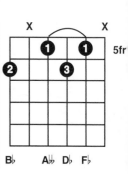

5fr

B♭ A♭♭ D♭ F♭

B (Bmaj)
B major

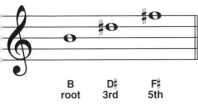

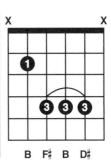

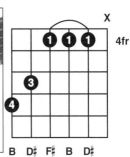

B5 (B(no 3rd))
B fifth (power chord)

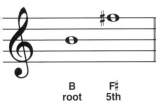

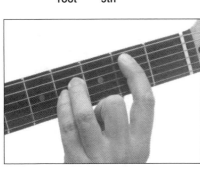

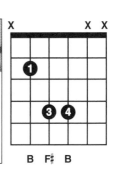

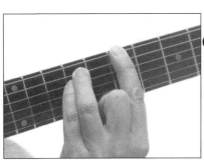

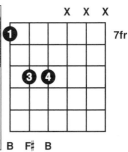

B

Bsus4 (Bsus)
B suspended fourth

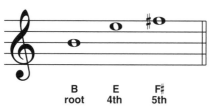

B | E | F#
root | 4th | 5th

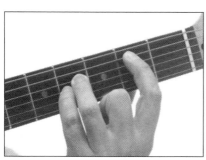
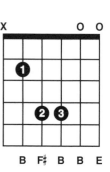

B F# B B E

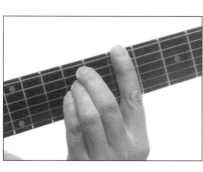
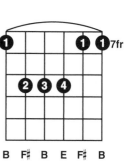

B F# B E F# B

Bsus2 (B5add2)
B suspended second

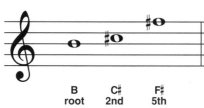

B | C# | F#
root | 2nd | 5th

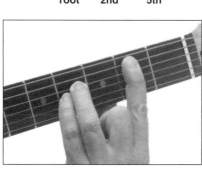
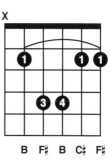

B F# B C# F#

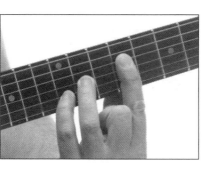
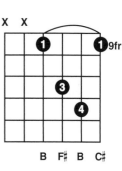

B F# B C#

Badd9

B added ninth

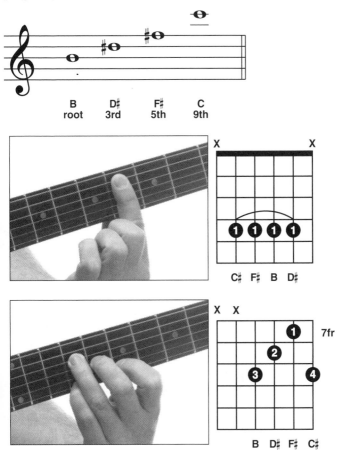

B	D#	F#	C
root	3rd	5th	9th

X   X

C#   F#   B   D#

X   X   7fr

B   D#   F#   C#

B6

B sixth

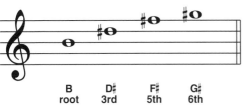

B	D#	F#	G#
root	3rd	5th	6th

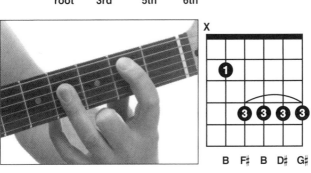

X

B   F#   B   D#   G#

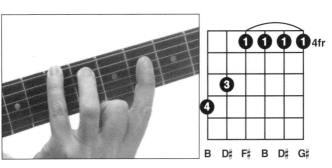

4fr

B   D#   F#   B   D#   G#

B

B6/9 (B6add9)

B sixth, added ninth

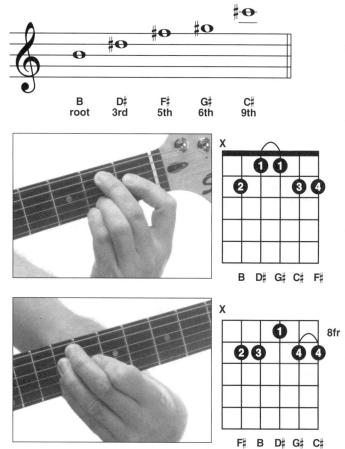

B	D#	F#	G#	C#
root	3rd	5th	6th	9th

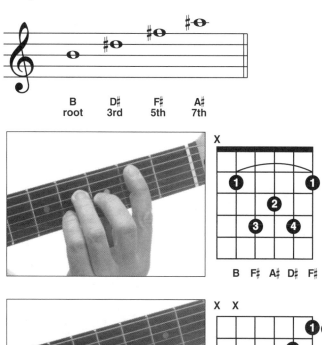

Bmaj7 (BM7)

B major seventh

B	D#	F#	A#
root	3rd	5th	7th

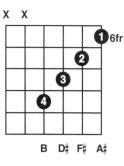

Bmaj9 (BM9)

B major ninth

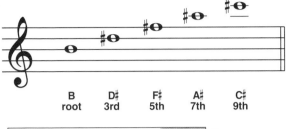

B	D#	F#	A#	C#
root	3rd	5th	7th	9th

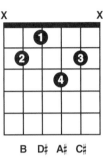

B D# A# C#

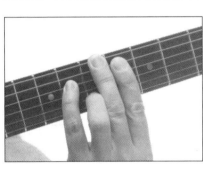

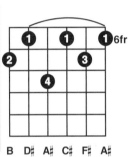

B D# A# C# F# A#

Bmaj7#11 (BM7#11)

B major seventh, sharp eleventh

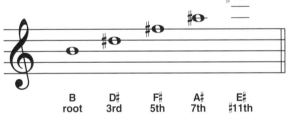

B	D#	F#	A#	E#
root	3rd	5th	7th	#11th

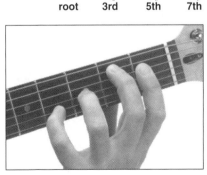

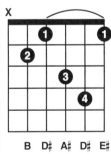

B D# A# D# E#

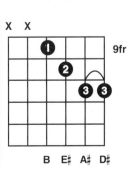

B E# A# D#

B

Bmaj13 (BM13)
B major thirteenth

B	D#	F#	A#	C#	G#
root	3rd	5th	7th	9th	13th

B F# A# D# G#

11fr

B D# G# A# D#

Bm (Bmin, B-)
B minor

B	D	F#
root	b3rd	5th

B F# B D F#

7fr

B F# B D F# B

Bm(add9)

B minor, added ninth

B	D	F#	C#
root	♭3rd	5th	9th

X X O

D B C# F#

9fr

D F# B C#

Bm6 (Bmin6, B-6)

B minor sixth

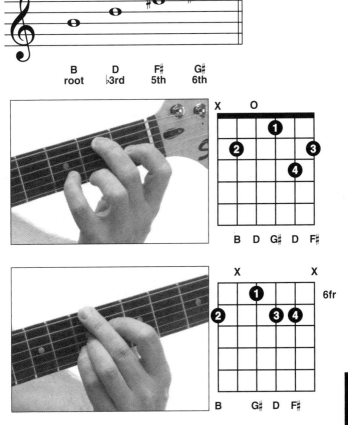

B	D	F#	G#
root	♭3rd	5th	6th

X O

B D G# D F#

X X

6fr

B G# D F#

B

Bm♭6 (B-(♭6), Bmin♭6)

B minor, flat sixth

B	D	F♯	G
root	♭3rd	5th	♭6th

B D G B F♯

B F♯ B D G

Bm6/9

B minor sixth, added ninth

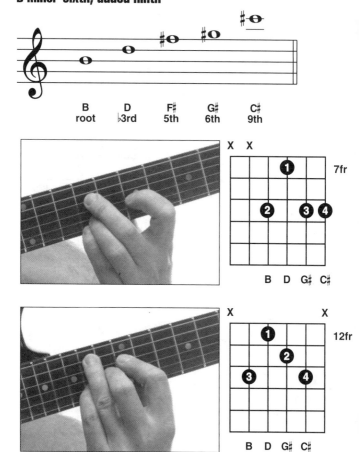

B	D	F♯	G♯	C♯
root	♭3rd	5th	6th	9th

7fr

B D G♯ C♯

12fr

B D G♯ C♯

Bm7 (B-7, Bmin7)
B minor seventh

B	D	F♯	A
root	♭3rd	5th	♭7th

Bm7♭5 (B-7♭5, Bmin7♭5)
B minor seventh, flat fifth

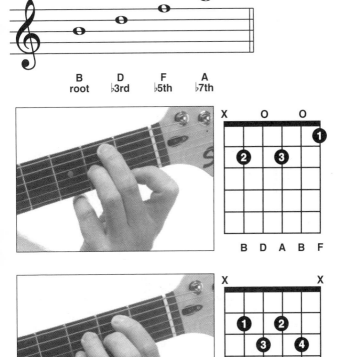

B	D	F	A
root	♭3rd	♭5th	♭7th

B

Bm(maj7) (B-(+7))
B minor, major seventh

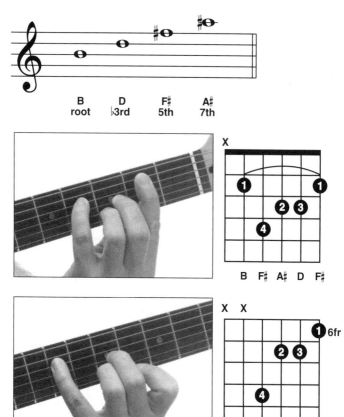

B	D	F#	A#
root	♭3rd	5th	7th

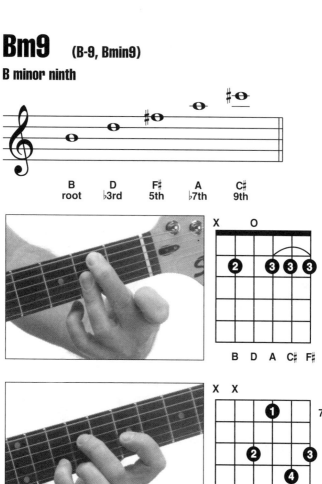

X

B F# A# D F#

X X

● 6fr

B D F# A#

Bm9 (B-9, Bmin9)
B minor ninth

B	D	F#	A	C#
root	♭3rd	5th	♭7th	9th

X O

B D A C# F#

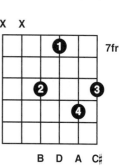

X X

7fr

B D A C#

Bm9♭5 (Bm9-5, Bmin9♭5)

B minor ninth, flat fifth

B	D	F	A	C#
root	♭3rd	♭5th	♭7th	9th

B D A C# F

7fr

B F A D A C#

Bm9(maj7) (Bm9+7, B-9+7)

B minor ninth, major seventh

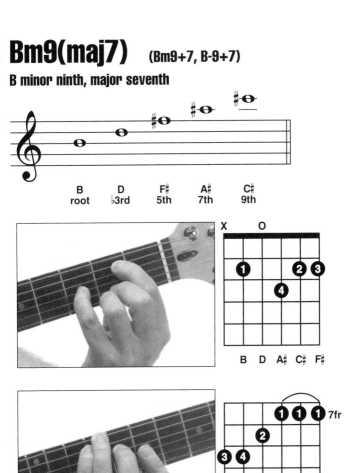

B	D	F#	A#	C#
root	♭3rd	5th	7th	9th

B D A# C# F#

7fr

C# F# A# D F# B

B

Bm11 (B-11, Bmin11)

B minor eleventh

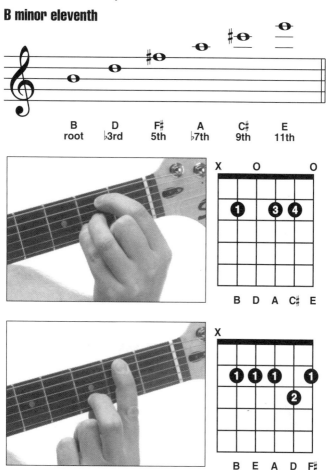

B	D	F#	A	C#	E
root	♭3rd	5th	♭7th	9th	11th

X O O

① ③ ④

B D A C# E

X

① ① ① ①

②

B E A D F#

Bm13 (B-13, Bmin13)

B minor thirteenth

B	D	F#	A	C#	G#
root	♭3rd	5th	♭7th	9th	13th

X

① ①

②

③ ④

B F# A D G#

X X

① ① 10fr

② ③

G# F# A D

B7 (Bdom7)
B dominant seventh

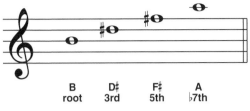

B	D#	F#	A
root	3rd	5th	♭7th

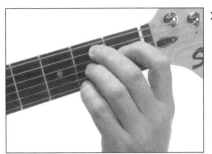
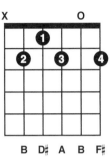

B D# A B F#

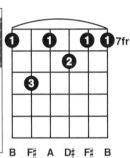

B F# A D# F# B

B7sus4 (B7sus)
B dominant seventh, suspended fourth

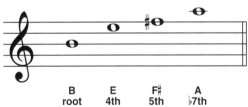

B	E	F#	A
root	4th	5th	♭7th

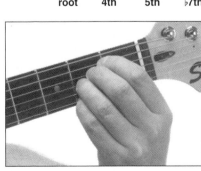
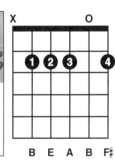

B E A B F#

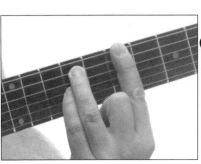
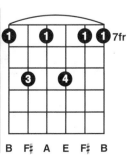

B F# A E F# B

B

B7♭5 (B7-5, Bdom7♭5)
B dominant seventh, flat fifth

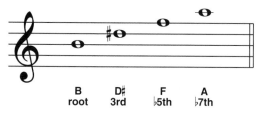

B	D#	F	A
root	3rd	♭5th	♭7th

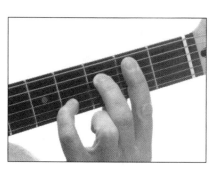

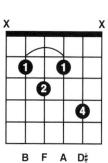

B9
B ninth

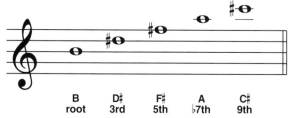

B	D#	F#	A	C#
root	3rd	5th	♭7th	9th

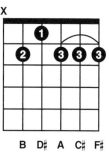

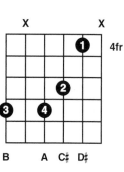

B9sus4 (B9sus)

B ninth, suspended fourth

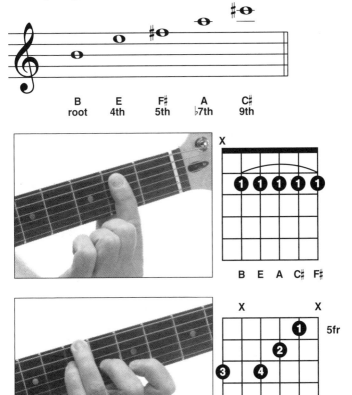

B	E	F#	A	C#
root	4th	5th	♭7th	9th

B E A C# F#

X X 5fr

B A C# E

B9♭5 (B9-5, Bdom9♭5)

B ninth, flat fifth

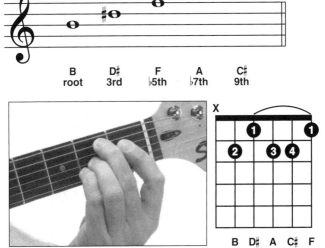

B	D#	F	A	C#
root	3rd	♭5th	♭7th	9th

B D# A C# F

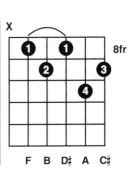

8fr

F B D# A C#

B

B7♭9 (B7-9, Bdom7♭9)
B dominant seventh, flat ninth

B	D♯	F♯	A	C
root	3rd	5th	♭7th	♭9th

B D♯ A C F♯

X · · · · X — 4fr

B   A C D♯

B7♯9 (B7+9, Bdom7♯9)
B dominant seventh, sharp ninth

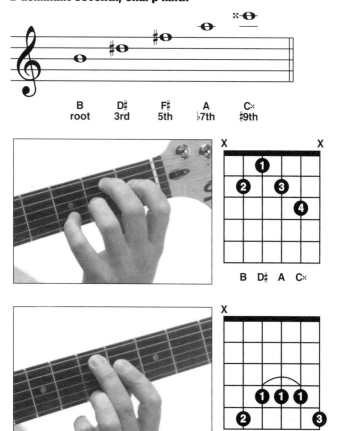

B	D♯	F♯	A	C𝄪
root	3rd	5th	♭7th	♯9th

B D♯ A C𝄪

C𝄪 F♯ B D♯ A

B7♭5(♯9) (B7-5(+9), Bdom7♭5(♯9))
B dominant seventh, flat fifth, sharp ninth

B	D♯	F	A	C𝄪
root	3rd	♭5th	♭7th	♯9th

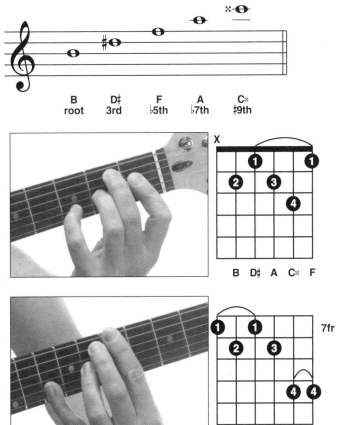

B D♯ A C𝄪 F

7fr

B F A D♯ A C𝄪

B11
B eleventh

B	D♯	F♯	A	C♯	E
root	3rd	5th	♭7th	9th	11th

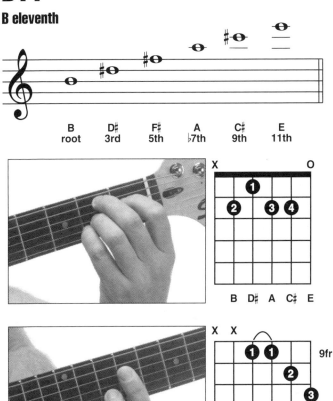

B D♯ A C♯ E

9fr

B E A D♯

B

B7♯11 (B7+11, Bdom7♯11)

B dominant seventh, sharp eleventh

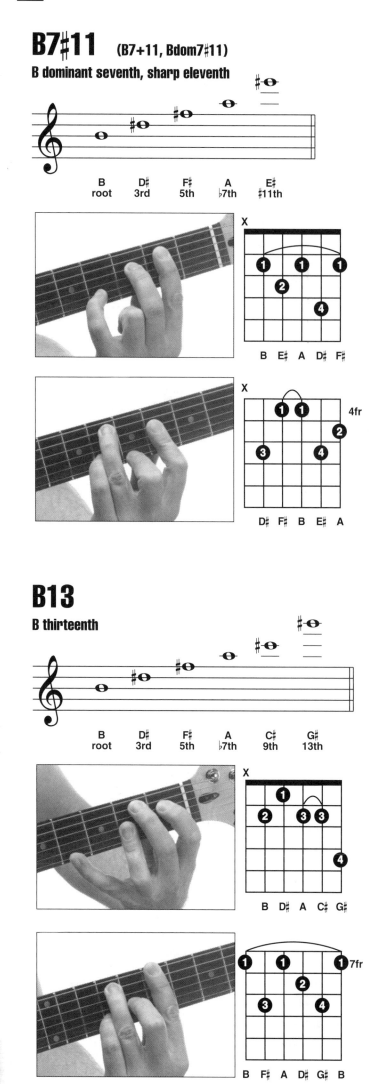

B	D♯	F♯	A	E♯
root	3rd	5th	♭7th	♯11th

B E♯ A D♯ F♯

4fr

D♯ F♯ B E♯ A

B13

B thirteenth

B	D♯	F♯	A	C♯	G♯
root	3rd	5th	♭7th	9th	13th

B D♯ A C♯ G♯

7fr

B F♯ A D♯ G♯ B

B13sus4 (B13sus)

B thirteenth, suspended fourth

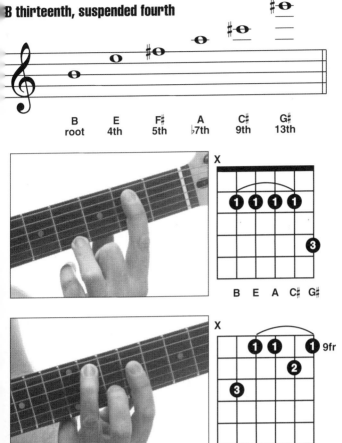

B	E	F#	A	C#	G#
root	4th	5th	♭7th	9th	13th

X

B E A C# G#

X

9fr

G# B E A C#

B+ (Baug, B(#5))

B augmented

B	D#	F𝄪
root	3rd	#5th

X   O   O

B D# F𝄪 B F𝄪

X X

7fr

B D# F𝄪 B

B

B+7 (B7#5)

B dominant seventh, sharp fifth

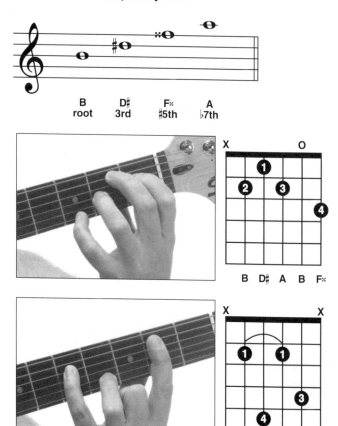

B	D#	F✕	A
root	3rd	#5th	♭7th

B D# A B F✕

B F✕ A D#

B° (Bdim)

B diminished

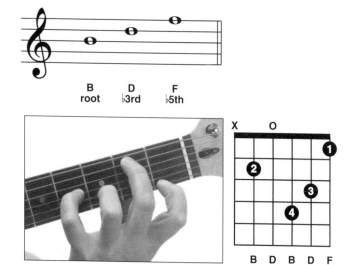

B	D	F
root	♭3rd	♭5th

B D B D F

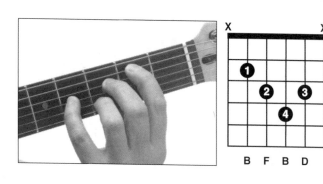

B F B D

B°7 (Bdim7)

B diminished seventh

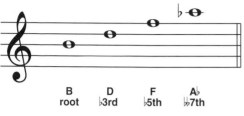

B	D	F	A♭
root	♭3rd	♭5th	♭♭7th

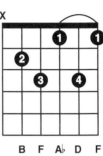

X

B F A♭ D F

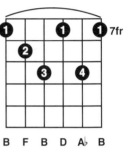

7fr

B F B D A♭ B